RHODES to LANGUAGE

by Anna Rhodes M.Ed., L.C.S.T.

Stass
PUBLICATIONS

Edited and Produced by STASS Publications
Parkside, Station Road, St. Mabyn
Cornwall, PL30 3BN
Tel: 01208 841450
email: info@stass.co.uk
www.stasspublications.co.uk

Printed by Field Print, Boldon Colliery, Tyne & Wear

ISBN 978-1-874534-31-0

CONTENTS

ACKNOWLEDGEMENTS

I would like to thank the children, their parents and my colleagues at Knowl Hill School, Pirbright, Surrey who have willingly tried out the games at different stages of development and offered constructive advice towards improvement.

I am very grateful to Mara Smit for her help in providing the original artwork used in part of the book.

Most importantly I would like to thank the many children I have worked with throughout my speech and language therapy career who have presented me with enough challenges to necessitate the development of these games.

INTRODUCTION

LANGUAGE

Language learning begins in infancy and continues throughout life. For the majority this is a skill which is acquired easily and naturally, but others may find it much more difficult for a variety of reasons. Difficulties with speech sounds or grammar are often easy to recognise but difficulties with language comprehension and use may be less obvious. Efficient language skills are the key to effective learning as they underpin all aspects of academic progress. It is now recognised that many children who struggle to achieve adequate levels of literacy often have an underlying difficulty with some aspects of language. Speech and language skills are also related to the social competence of an individual.

Rhodes to Language provides games to allow for learning in a relaxed and natural environment. The games are each designed to address specific areas of language use and also allow practice of social behaviours such as concentrating, listening, taking turns and following rules. They are based on the National Curriculum at Key Stages 1 and 2. Games with dice also encourage counting, sequencing and directional awareness such as left, right, up and down. The game boards on pages 12 and 58 also allow for probability to be discussed.

The games have been used successfully with children from 7 - 16 years in both individual and group settings in a special school. Originally developed for dyslexic children, they also offer a practical and flexible resource for both schools and clinics for a wide range of people, including children with delayed language development, learning difficulties, and also adults, who need to develop language skills.

The book is designed to be a flexible resource and blank cards have been included to allow for additional or topical items to be added. The games can be photocopied to provide homework packages. It is suggested that the game boards are enlarged to A3 size and laminated.

The Pirate, Fantasy, Space, Football and Safari games are available as laminated boards in FULL COLOUR from STASS Publications in A3 size (approx. 41cms x, 29cms) or A2 size (approx. 58.5 cms x 41cms). A Game Pack is also available containing dice, shaker, counters, spinner and an egg timer). Telephone 01661 822316 for details.

Group Them

Aim: The object of the game is to help children to group nouns into different categories.

Materials: Photocopy either pages 4 - 6 (pictures) or 7 - 9 (text) onto card and cut along the dotted lines. Laminate if possible.
A board game from the back of the book.

Game: Place the cards in a pile face down on the table. The players take turns to turn over a card and name a category for the items on the card. Players then can throw the dice and move round the board game.

A page of blank cards has been included on page 10 so that additional categories may be added as required.

Players can be encouraged to think of other items which could be included in the categories.

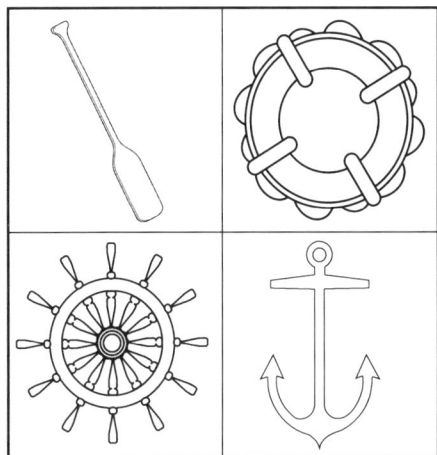

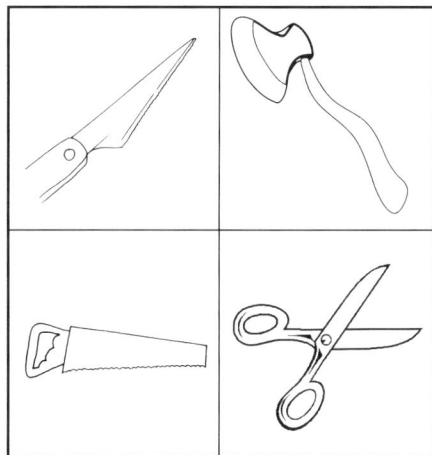

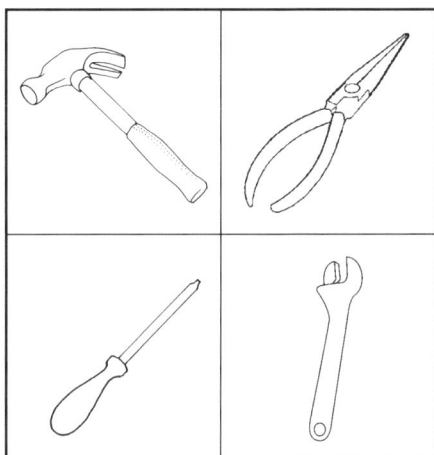

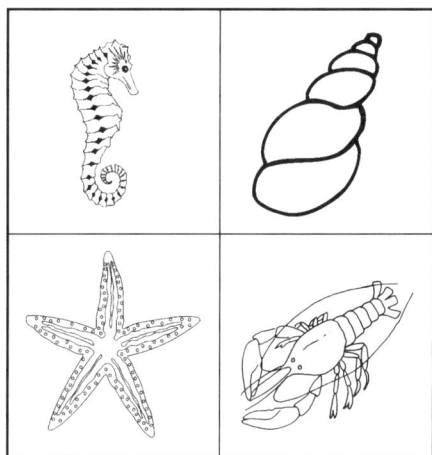

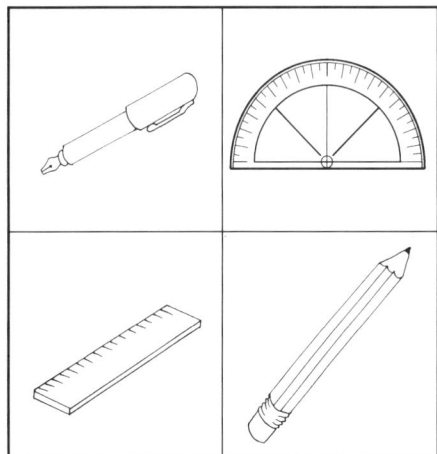

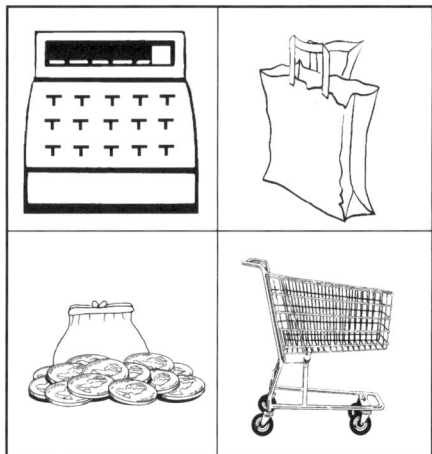

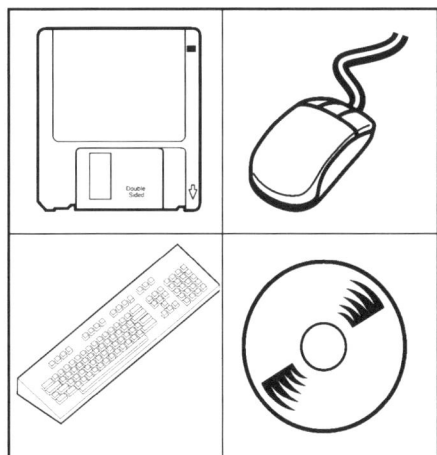

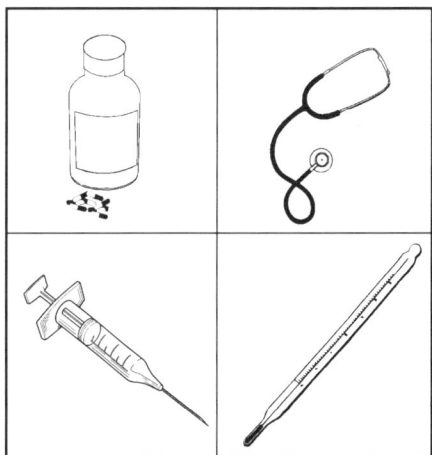

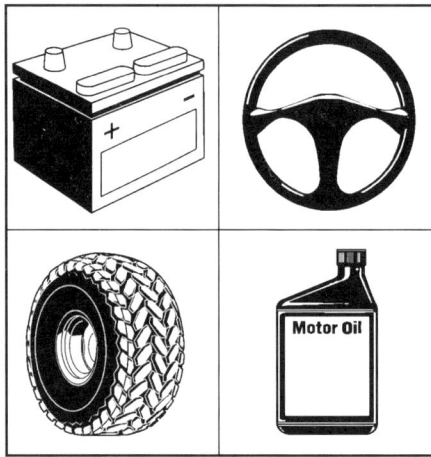

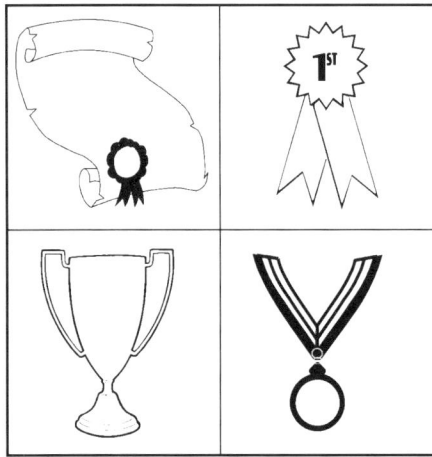

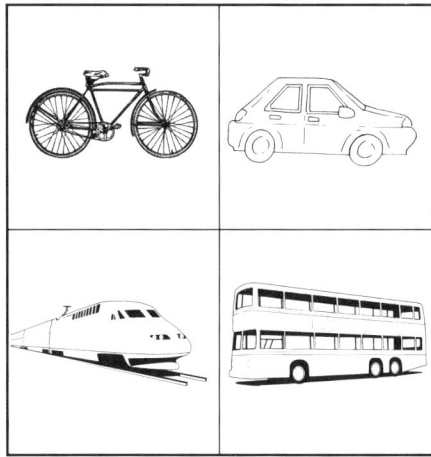

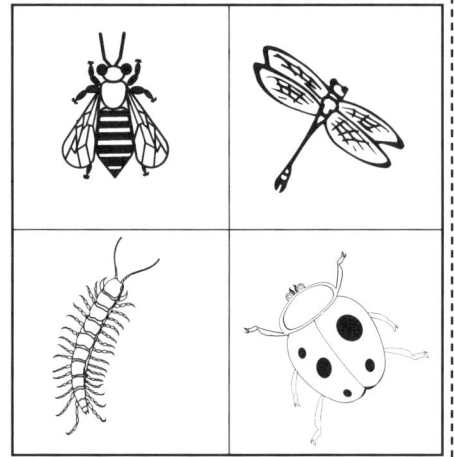

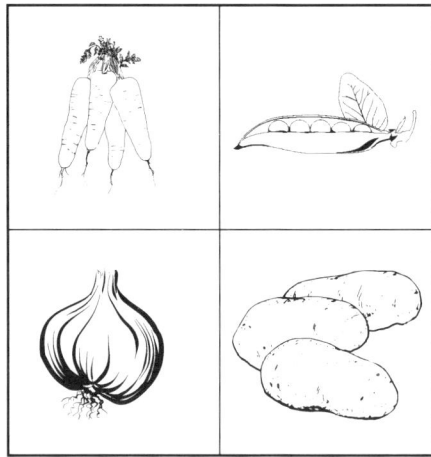

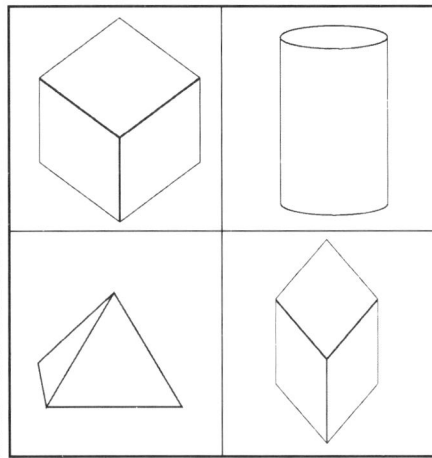

oak birch willow larch	shirt trousers hat skirt
red blue black orange	plum banana pear pineapple
daisy rose tulip daffodil	pen pencil ruler crayon
spoon knife fork teaspoon	bowl plate cup saucer
bed table chair wardrobe	bee wasp fly moth
cow goat pig sheep	owl sparrow robin thrush

cod salmon trout haddock	school hospital house shop
boots slippers shoes sandals	piano violin harp guitar
golf football rugby tennis	carrot turnip potato parsnip
tea coffee milk coke	chisel hammer saw drill
silk satin wool cotton	tea dinner lunch breakfast
cap hood helmet bonnet	March October June May

happy　　angry sad　　anxious	aunt　　father nephew　sister
Neptune　Mars Jupiter　　Saturn	duster　mop polish　dustpan
he　　them her　　us	noun　　adjective verb　　pronoun
hoe　　spade trowel　shears	who　　how when　　where
snow　　rain fog　　sleet	captain　private general　sergeant
lake　　stream river　　sea	Mirror　Sun Times　Telegraph

Naming Nouns

Aim: The object of the game is to encourage the naming of members of different categories of nouns.

Materials: A dice.
6 counters per player.
Photocopy pages 14 - 17 onto card and cut along the dotted lines. Laminate if possible. Make enough copies of page 12 so that each player has a copy of the ladders, or use one sheet and only 6 counters for the whole group.

Game: The aim of the game is to see which ladder is completed first. Set out the ladders with a counter at the foot of each. Place the cards face down in a pile in the middle of the table. Players take it in turns to throw the dice and turn over a card to reveal a category. They then have to name the number of members of a category as shown on the dice:
 e.g. throw a 5, turn over 'animals' and name 5 animals.
The counter is then moved up one rung of ladder 5.
The concept of probability can be explored using the ladder game, i.e. which number has been used most often in the game, and which number (if any) has not been used in the game.

Alternatively play a board game at the end of the book. The player names 6 members of the category before throwing the dice and moving round the board.

A page of blank cards has been included on page 18 for additional categories.

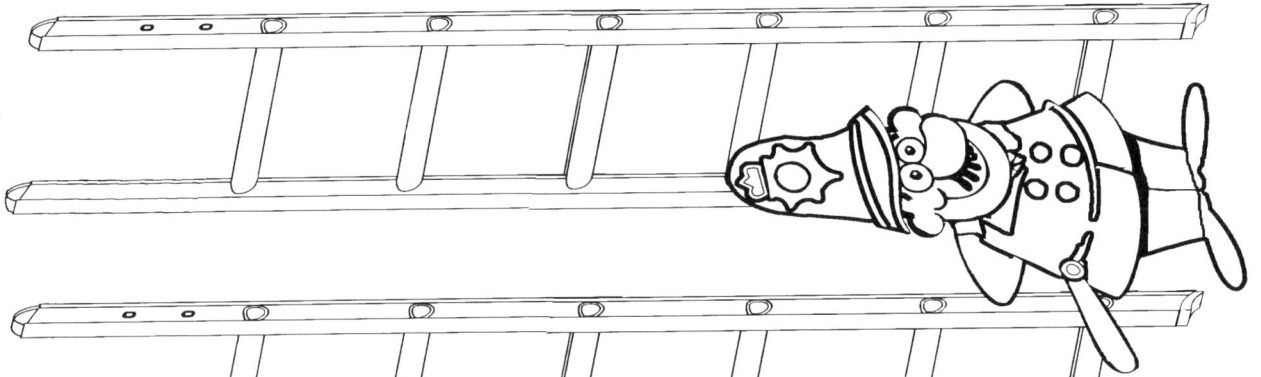

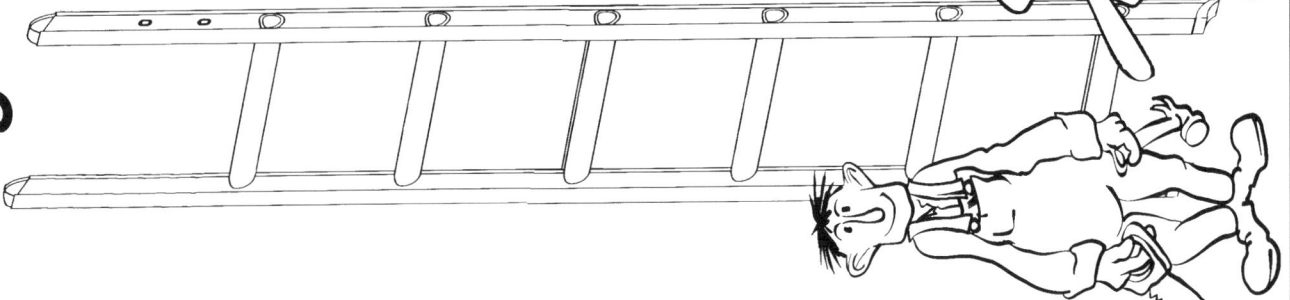

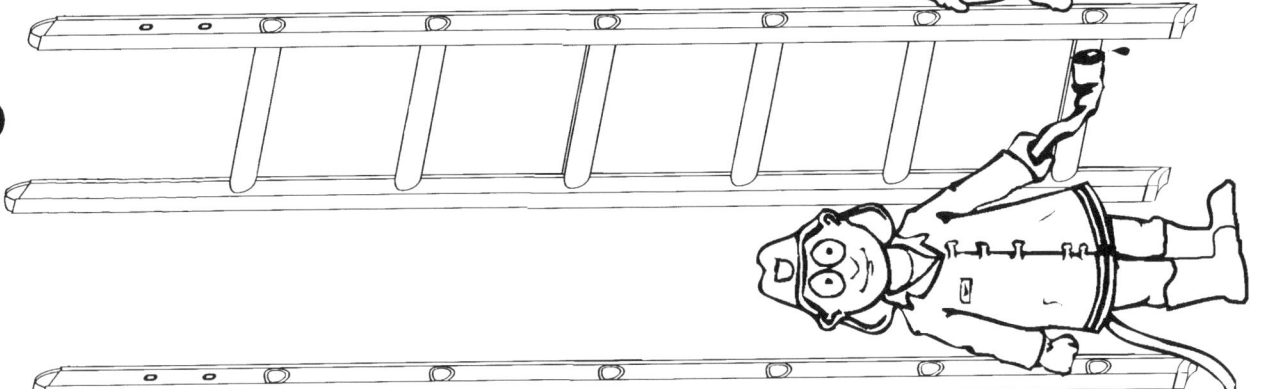

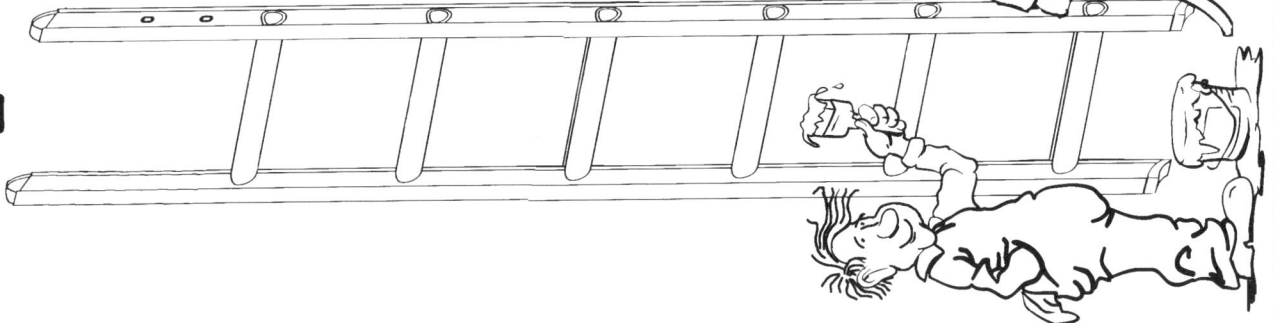

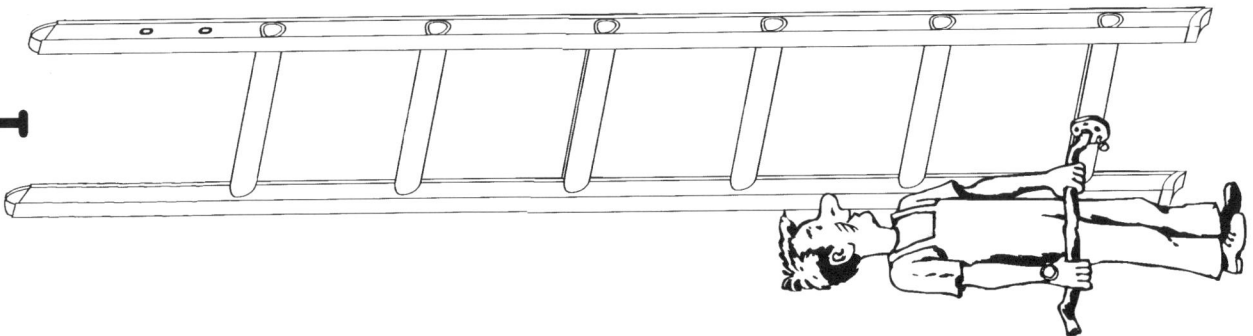

Speed Naming

Aim: To increase the speed of word retrieval within a given category.

Materials: A one minute egg timer.
                  Photocopy pages 14 - 17, onto card and cut along the dotted lines. Laminate if possible.

Game: Players take it in turns to turn over a card to reveal a category. They turn over the timer and name as many items as they can within the category in the set time. Give help as required. Encourage self and peer monitoring by listening for repetitions.
                  This can be played in conjunction with one of the game boards at the back of the book.

A page of blank cards has been included on page 18 so that additional categories may be added as required.

pets

shops

footwear

cartoon characters

Pop groups

TV programmes

electrical items

animals with horns

birds

fish

flowers

insects

stationery

countries

hobbies

buildings

things that swim

things that fly

things that grow

people who
wear uniforms

school subjects

things found at
the seaside

things found in
the park

things
you can read

things found

in a town

things found

on a farm

things made

of wood

things made

of metal

things that

will float

things that

will sink

things that

are tall

things found

underground

things that

are shiny

things found

in school

things you

can sail in

things that

use a motor

things that
you like

things that you
don't like

things made
of plastic

things made
of glass

things made
of wool

things you
can smell

things that
are sharp

things that
are soft

things that
are cold

things that
are hot

things that
are hard

things that
are round

Noun Lotto

Aim: The object of the game is to recognise which items belong in a particular category.

Materials: Photocopy pages 21 - 25 onto card and cut along the dotted lines. Laminate if possible.
Photocopy the board on page 20 for each player.

Game: Give each player a board and deal out 6 cards face down to each player. Place the rest of the cards face down in the centre of the table. Players look at their cards and choose which category they are going to collect. Any cards they hold which belong to that category they can place on their boards, the rest they hold in their hands. Players then take it in turns to pick a card from the pile in the centre and discard one card from their hands. Any cards which belong in their category can be placed on their board. The winner is the player who completes their board first.

Players should be encouraged to verbalise during the game, i.e. *This is a fruit but I am collecting wild animals so I'll throw it away.*

A page of blank cards has been included on page 26 so that additional pictures may be added as required.

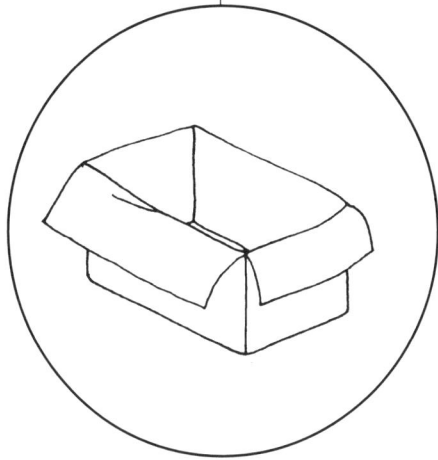

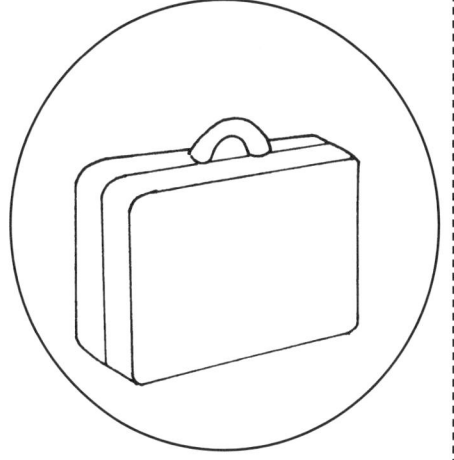
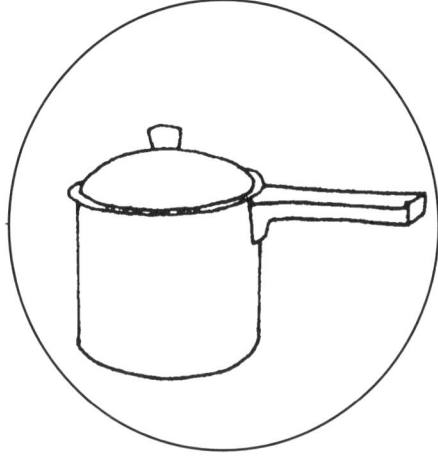

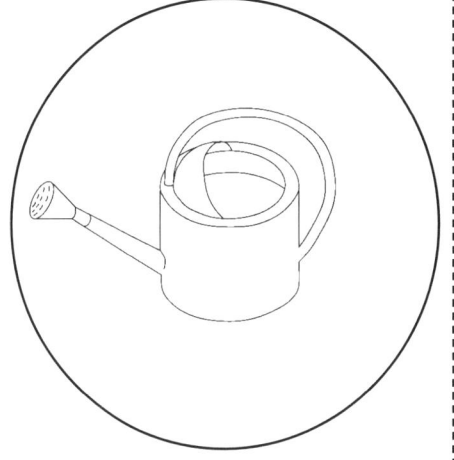

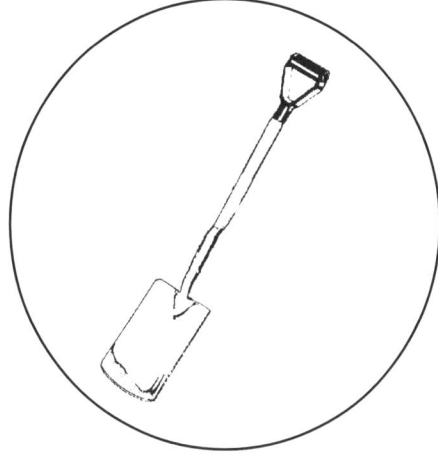
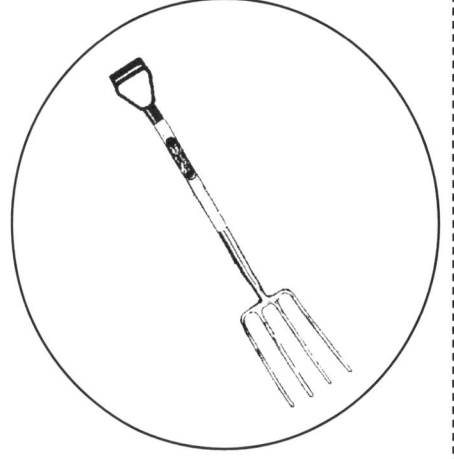

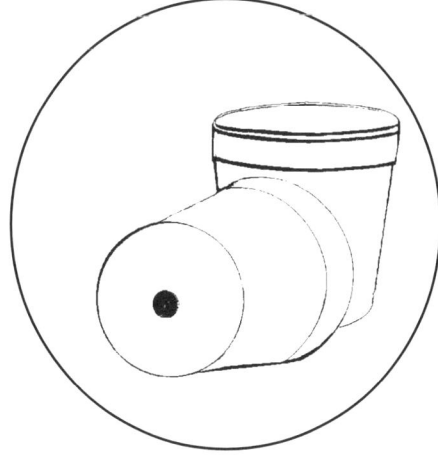
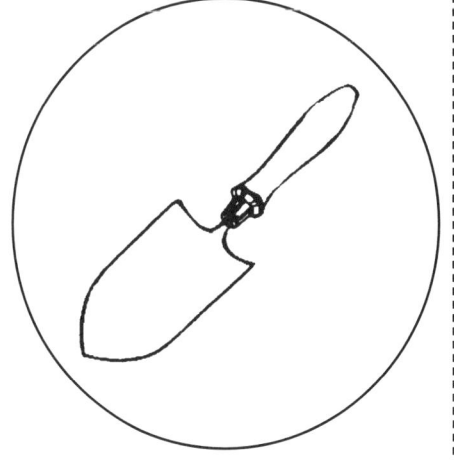

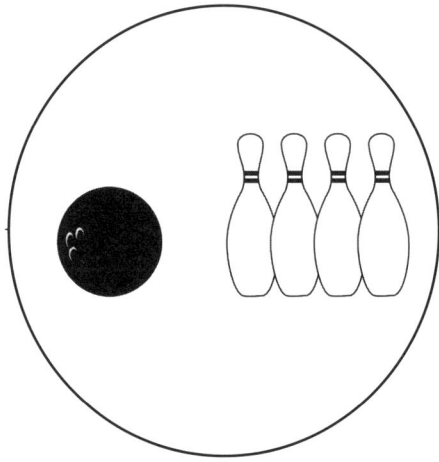

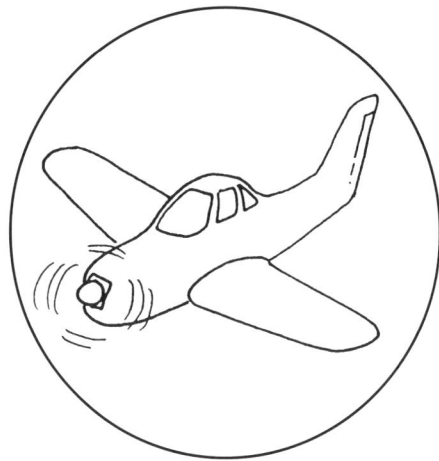

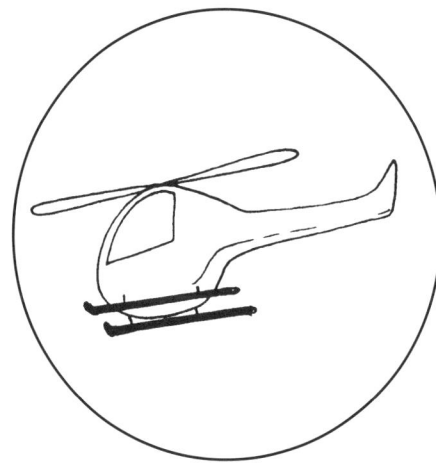

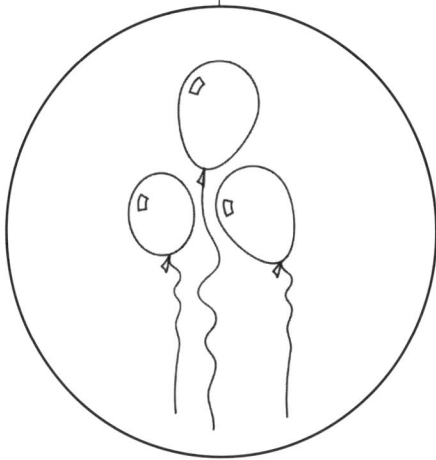
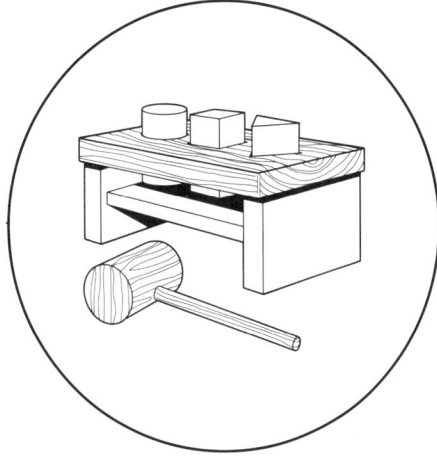
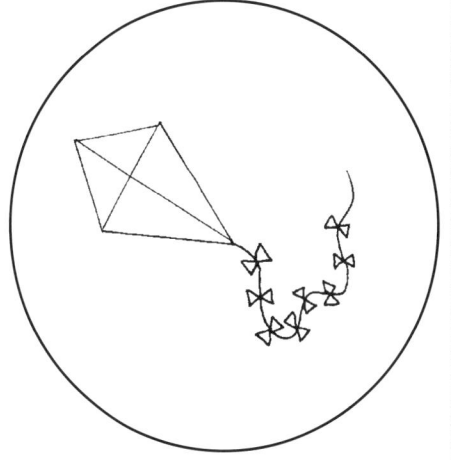

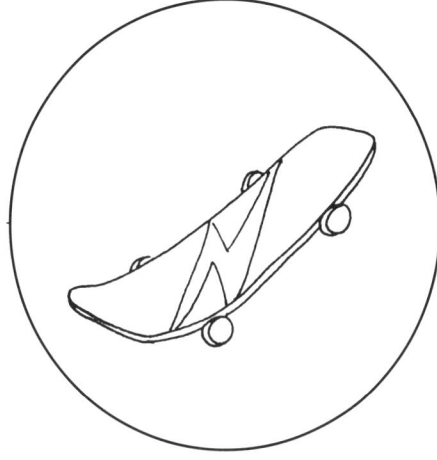

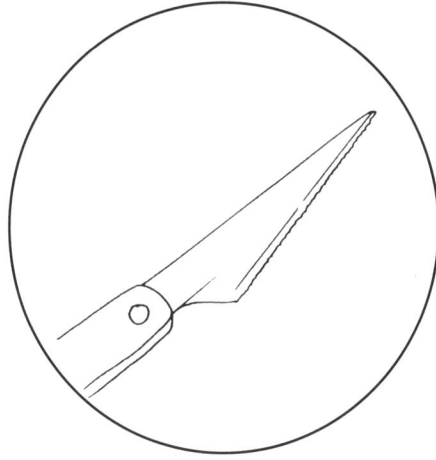
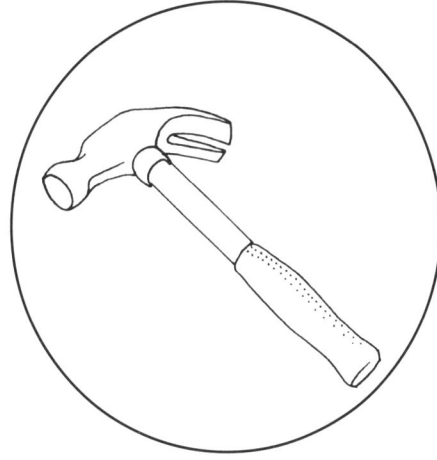
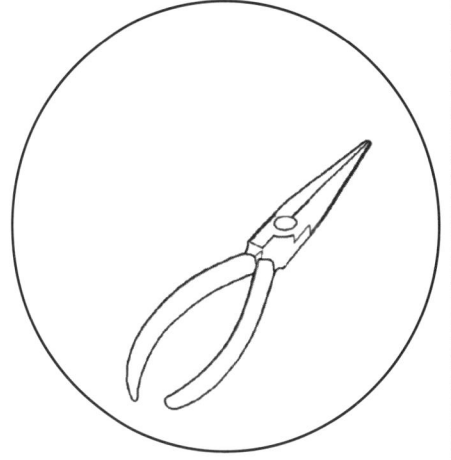
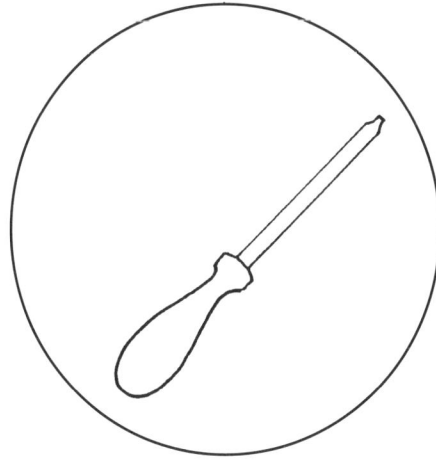
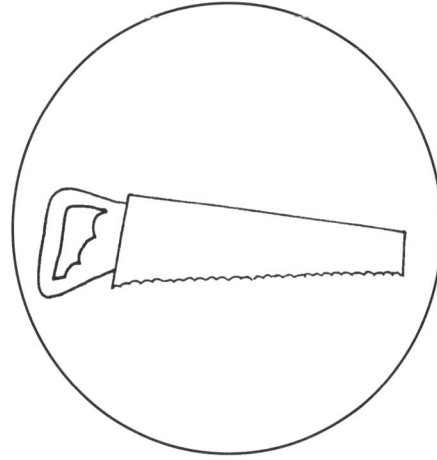

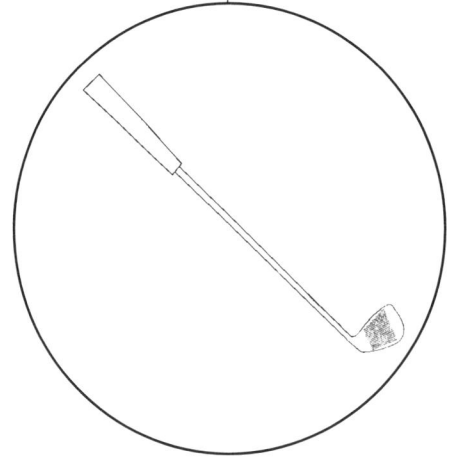

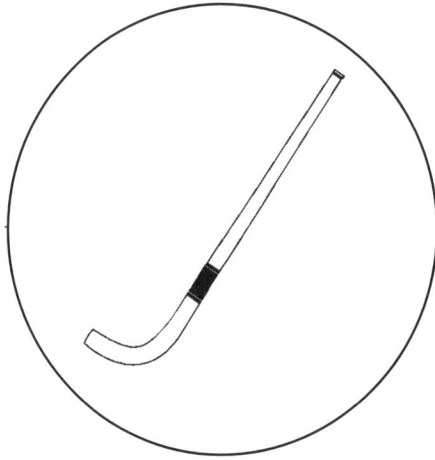

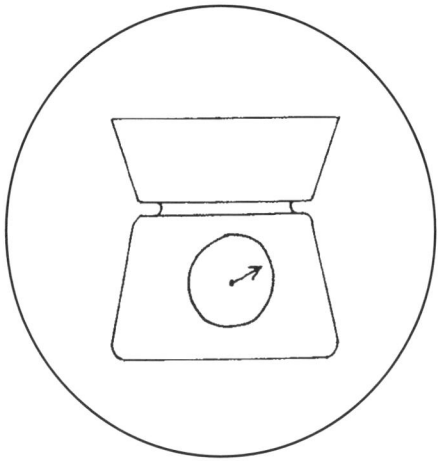
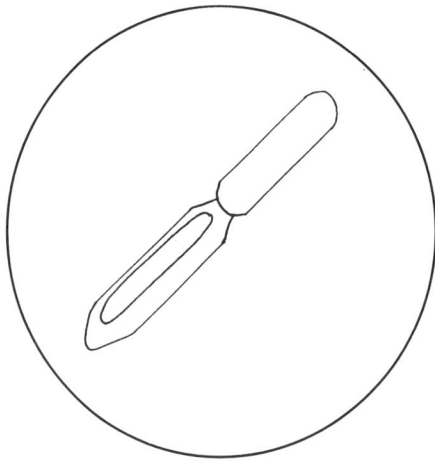
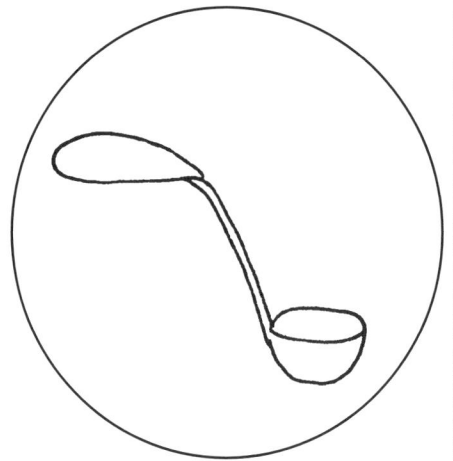

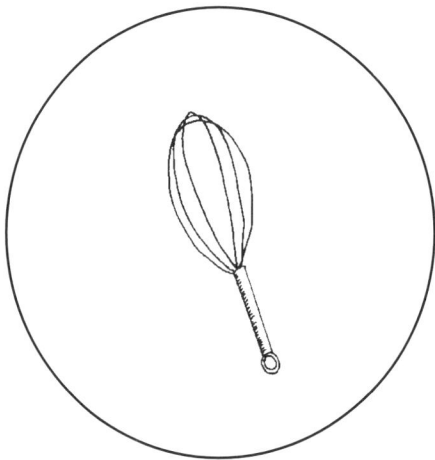
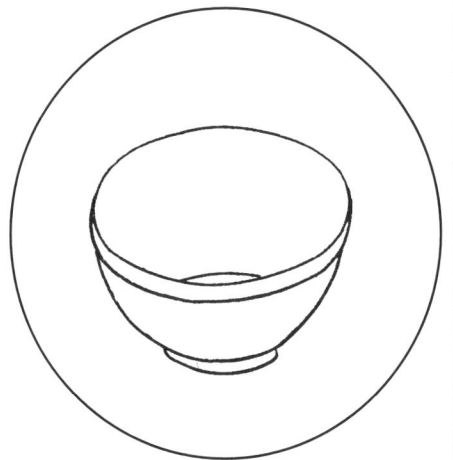

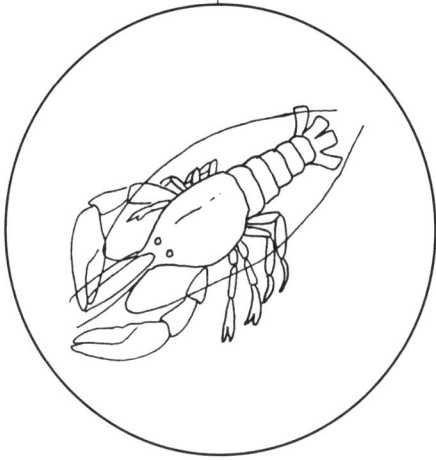

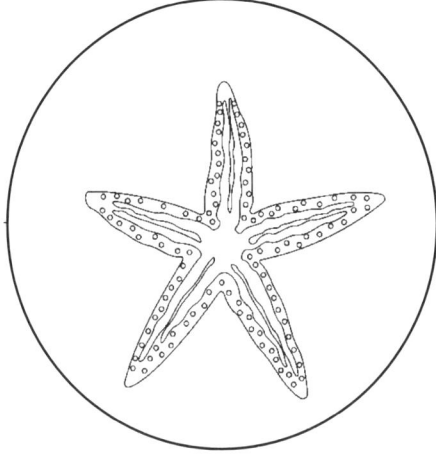

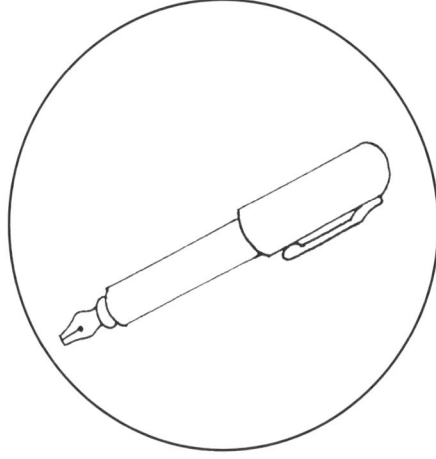
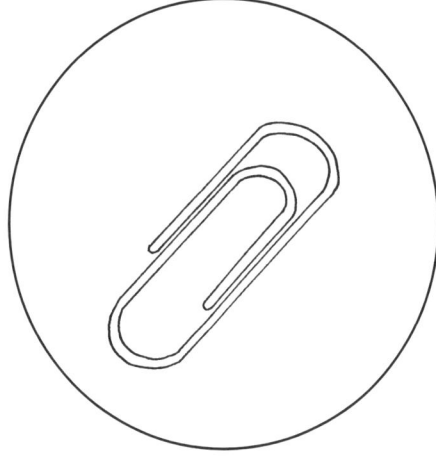
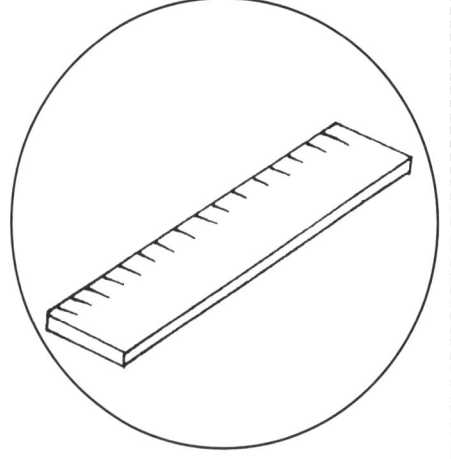

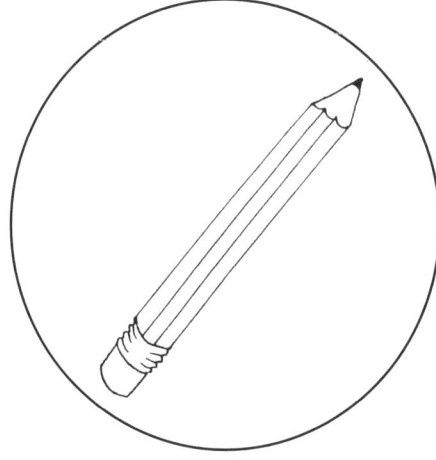
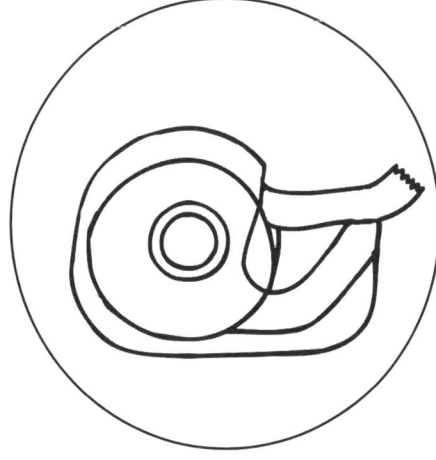
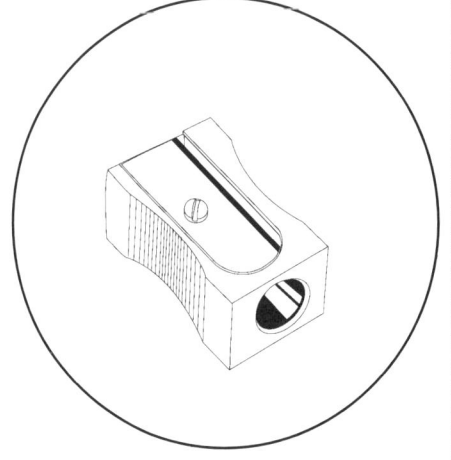

Odd One Out

27

Aim: The object of the game is find which item does not belong in the same category as the other three.

Materials: Photocopy either pages 28 - 30 (pictures) or 31 - 33 (text) onto card and cut along the dotted lines. Laminate if possible.

Game: Place the cards face down in a pile on the table. Players take it in turns to pick a card and name the odd one out. Encourage the player to explain their choice,
e.g. *it's the starfish because all the others can fly and it can't fly.*

A page of blank cards has been included on page 34 for additional items.

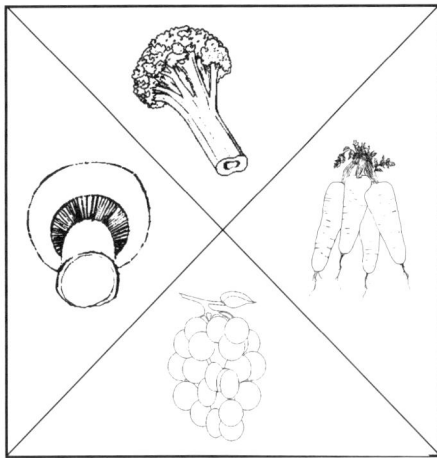

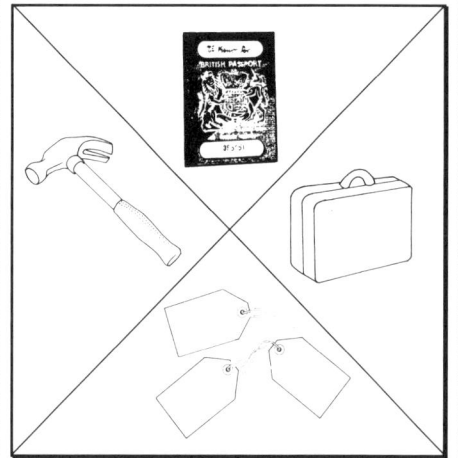

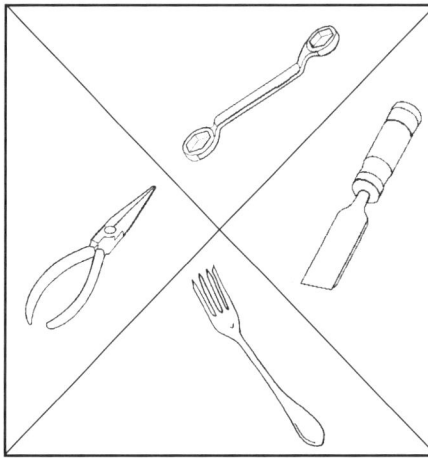

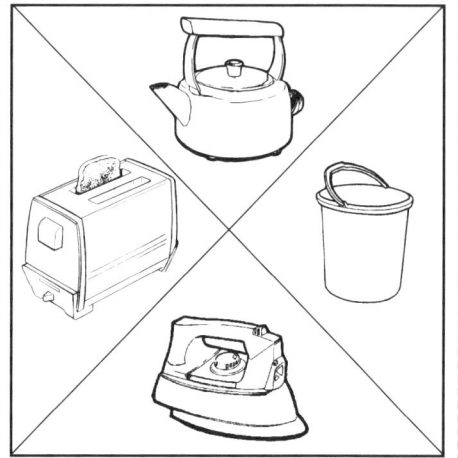

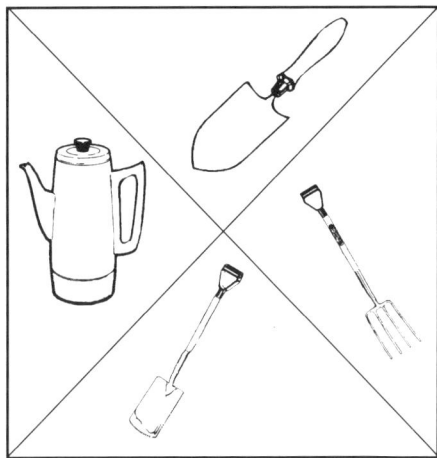

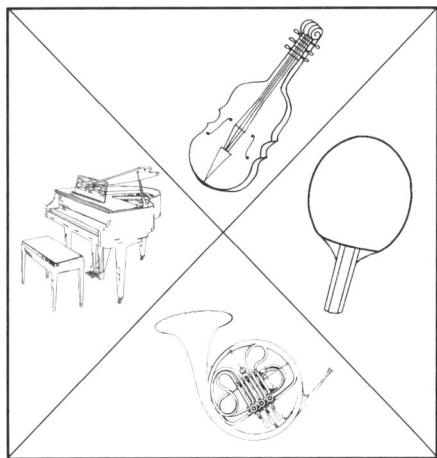

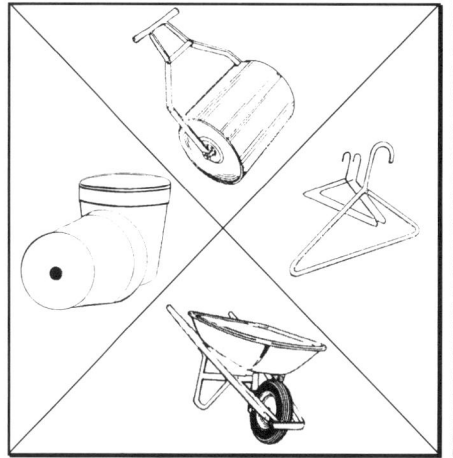
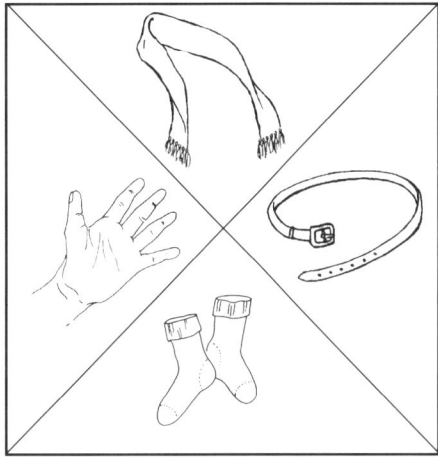

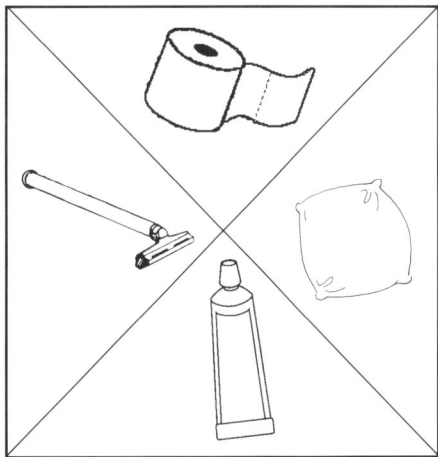

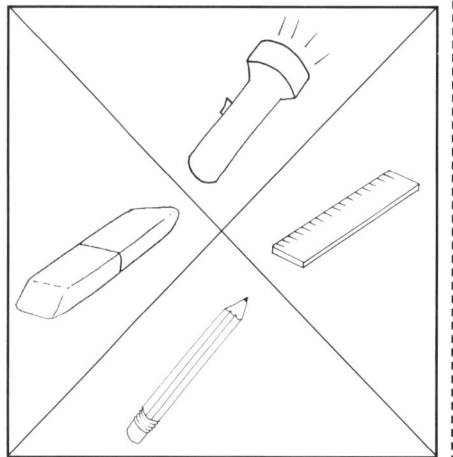

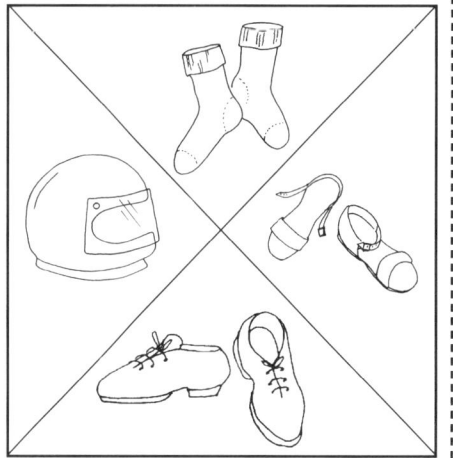

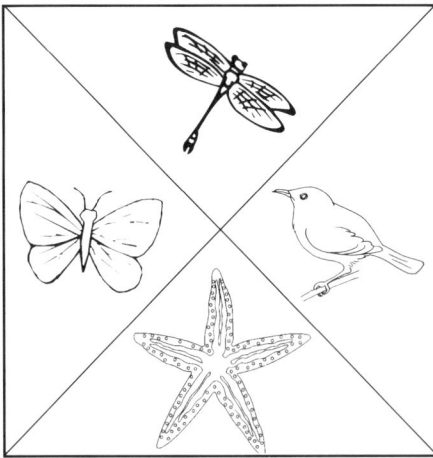

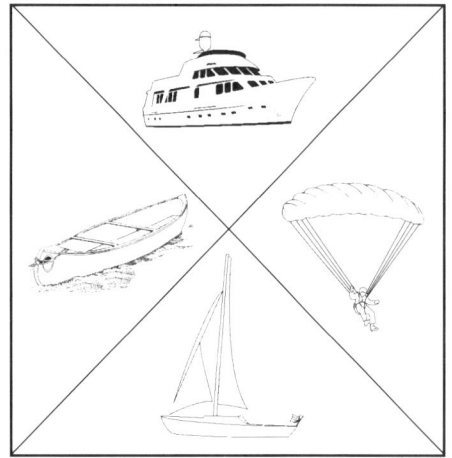

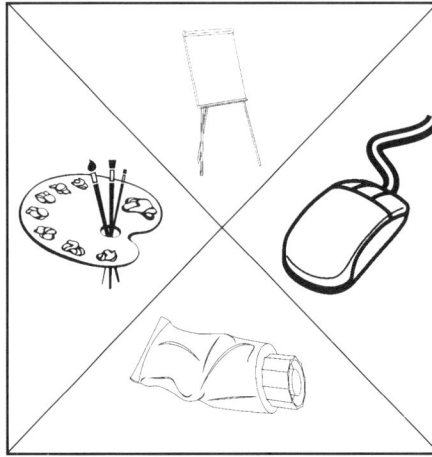
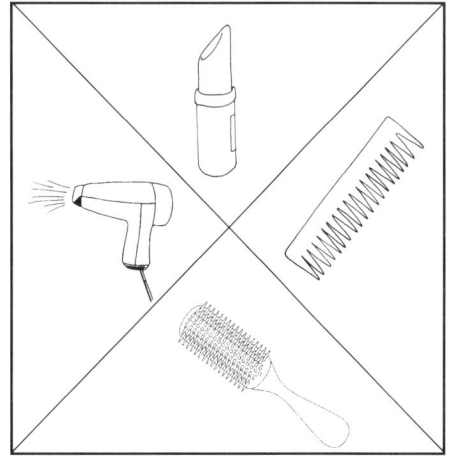
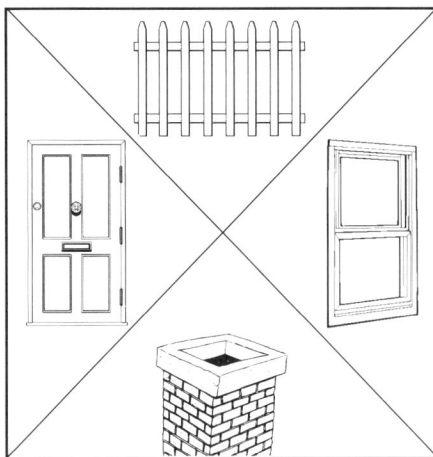
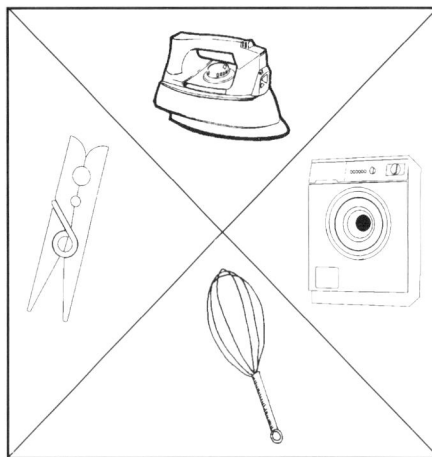
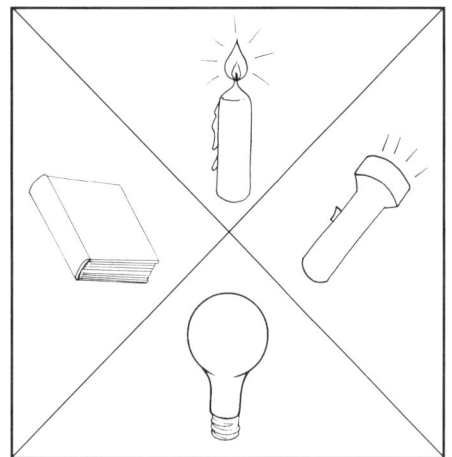
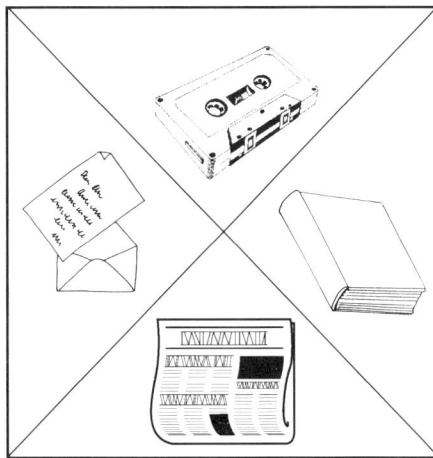
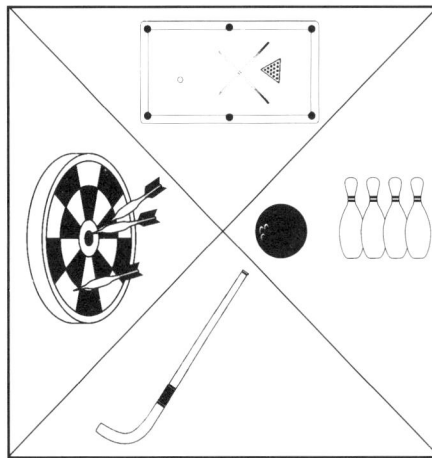
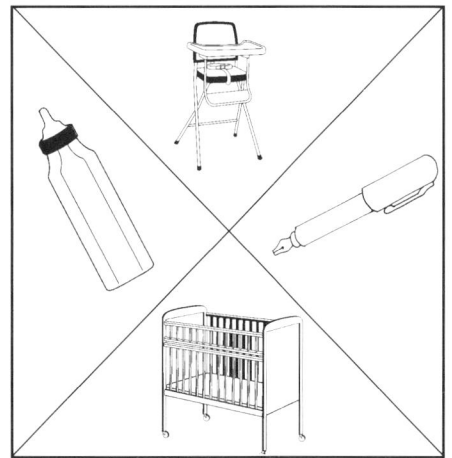

daisy grass rose daffodil	horse cow bee dog
green red yellow bright	ball doll stone teddy
spoon chisel saw hammer	plum rose apple cherry
car bus taxi bicycle	piano violin ball trumpet
milk lemonade cake water	shirt tent coat hat
cod seagull trout herring	nail chair stool wardrobe

cup	saucer	table	roof
plate	fork	chair	bed

church	house	rocket	mars
barn	wall	venus	pluto

yacht	canoe	coffee	tea
lorry	ferry	milk	bread

shoes	slippers	Italy	London
laces	boots	France	Spain

shell	cow	book	magazine
crab	sand	picture	newspaper

spoon	knife	paper	wood
axe	scissors	glass	box

brooch necklace ring lipstick	town village house city
Winter Easter Autumn Summer	bee grasshopper bird butterfly
melon carrot turnip cabbage	pencil crayon pen ruler
beef potato lamb chicken	television fridge freezer cooker
passport work suitcase tickets	spade leaf stem roots
Bob John Mary Bill	rain snow hail cloud

Compound Words

Aim: The object of the game is to combine two words into one compound word.

Materials: Photocopy either pages 36 - 38 (pictures) or 39 - 41 (text) depending on the level required, onto card and cut along the dotted lines. Laminate if possible

Game: Give each player six cards either from the beginning or end of the compound words. Place the other cards in a pile face down on the table. Players take it in turns to pick up one card and see if it will make a compound word with any of their cards. If not it is put on a discard pile and the next player has the chance to pick a new card from the pack or from the discard pile.

A page of blank cards has been included on page 42 so that players can be encouraged to add more items.

Picture Compound Words:

armchair	bagpipes	football	fortnight	peanut	penknife
bookcase	bookworm	goldfish	handbag	raincoat	sandshoes
buttercup	butterfly	headlamp	keyboard	signpost	snowman
cheesecake	cowboy	ladybird	letterbox	starfish	sunflower
dragonfly	eggcup	lighthouse	lipstick	sunglasses	sunhat
earphone	earring	moonlight	netball	tshirt	teaspoon
earwig	flowerpot	notebook	pancake	toenail	wheelchair

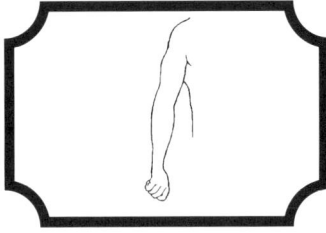 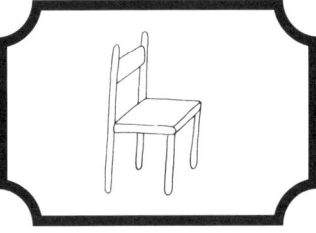 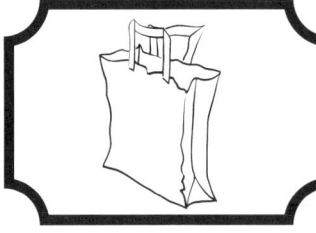 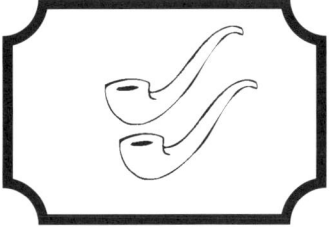

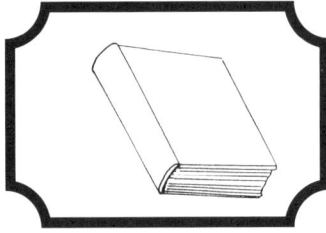 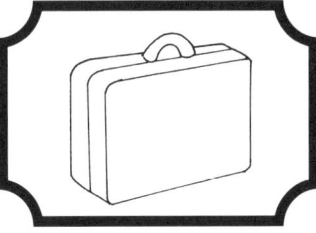 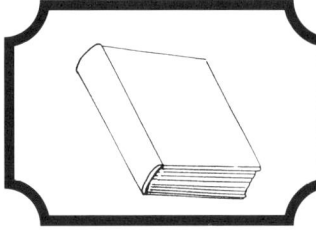 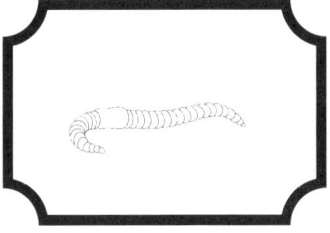

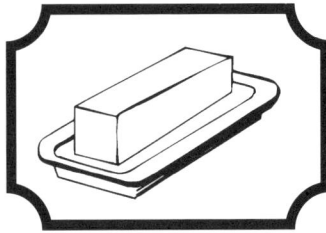  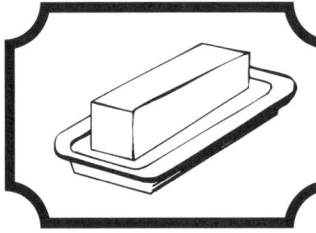 

  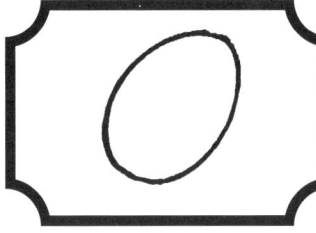 

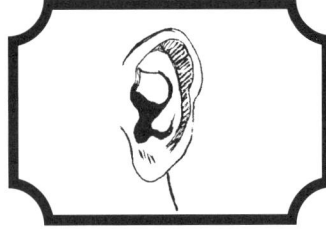   

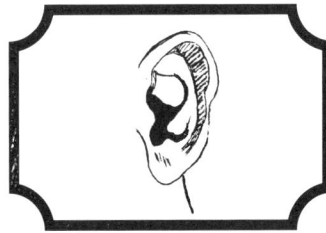   

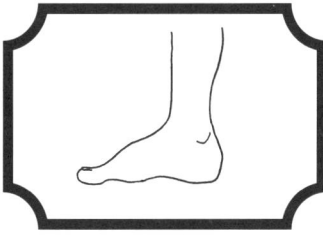
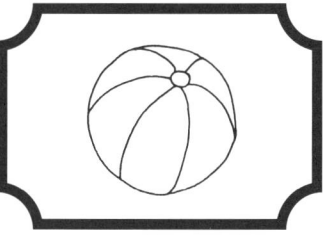

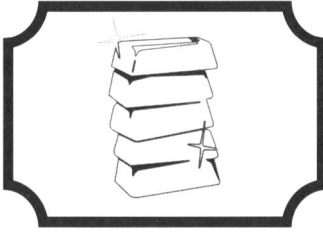
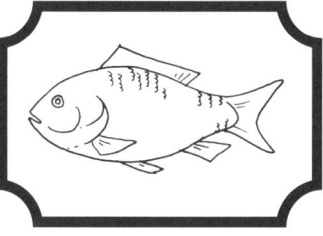
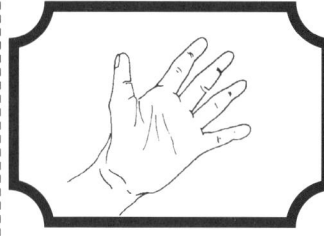
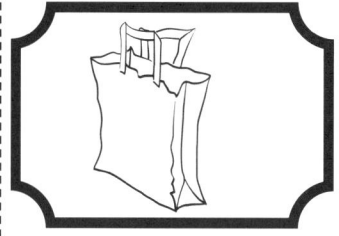

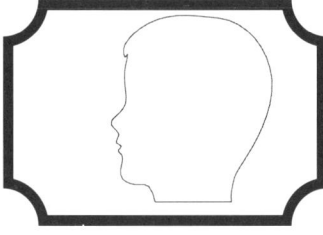
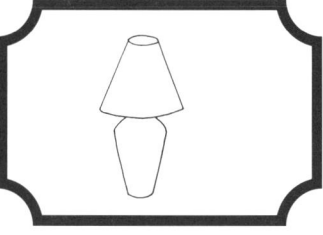
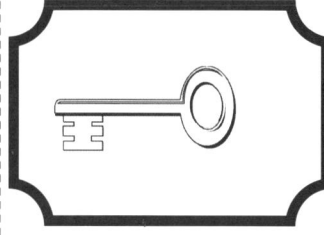

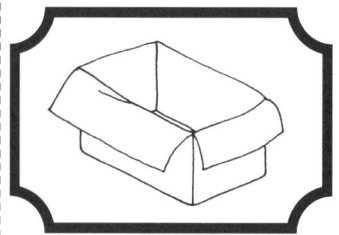

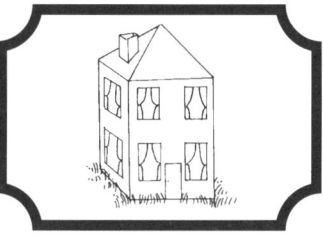

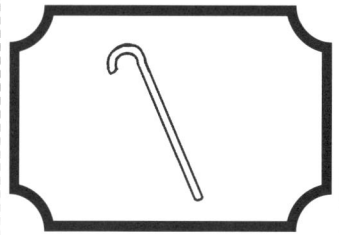

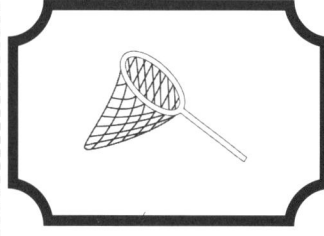
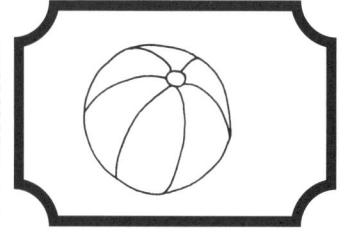

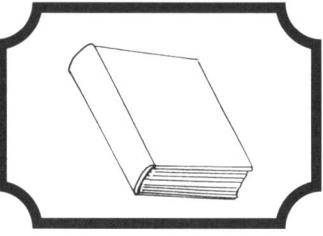
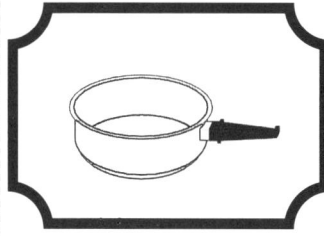

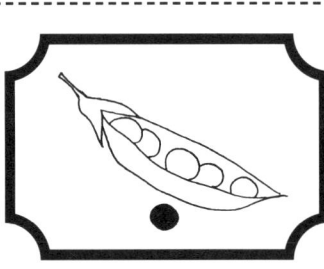

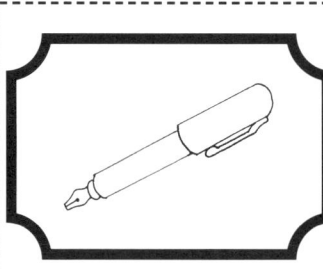
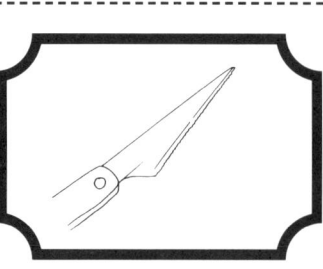

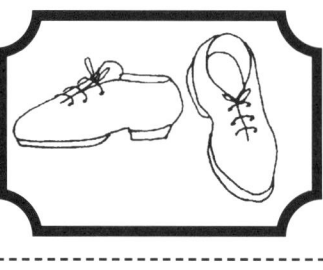
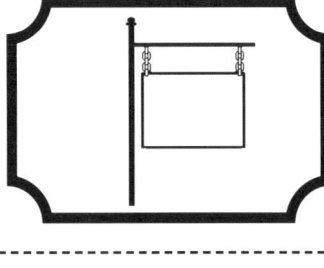

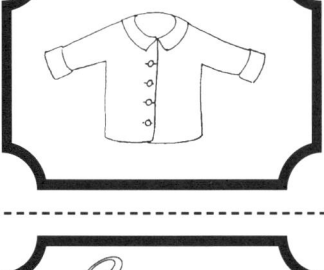

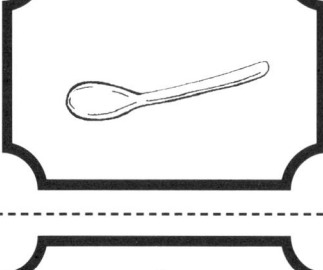
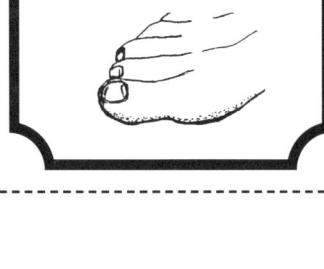
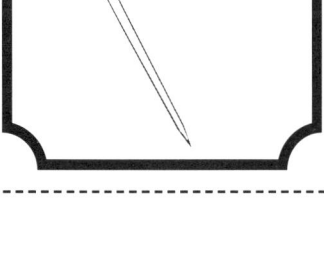

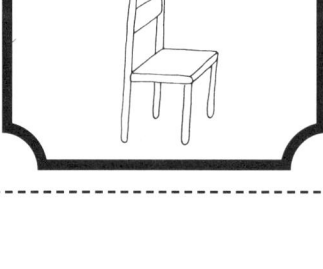

arm	chair	bath	room
birth	day	break	fast
cat	nap	corn	flakes
cross	word	drain	pipe
earth	quake	grape	fruit
goose	berry	hair	brush
hair	cut	hand	shake

head	ache	high	light
home	work	jig	saw
key	board	knock	out
light	bulb	light	house
lip	stick	May	day
milk	shake	night	dress
note	book	over	coat

play	ground	sand	shoes
sea	side	sight	see
stair	case	sun	flower
super	market	sweat	shirt
table	cloth	table	tennis
tea	bag	tea	spoon
track	suit	wind	mill

Word Play

Aim: The object of the game is to find one word which will form two different words when combined with the words on the word line, i.e. *cup* will form both *eggcup* and *cupboard.*

Materials: Photocopy pages 44 - 49 onto card and cut along the dotted lines. Laminate if possible

Game: Each player is given a base card.

a) Shuffle the small cards and place in the centre of the table. Players take turns to take a card from the pile and try to fit it into their base card. If it does not fit, it is put face up in a discard pile. The next player can either take a new card from the pile, or the card from the discard pile.

b) Lay out the small cards face down on the table (as in Pelmanism). Players take it in turns to turn over a card and try to fit it into their base card. If it does not fit, it is returned to its place face down on the table. This encourages visual memory and concentration skills as the players must pay attention throughout the game.

A page of blank cards has been included on page 50 so that more items can be added.

egg	board

scare	bar

saw	bin

note	case

cup

crow

dust

book

ice		bun

over		hanger

good		mare

fore		ache

cream   coat

night   head

sign ⬡ man

car ⬡ pipe

lolly ⬡ music

day ⬡ bulb

post

horn

pop

light

news | boy

sun | time

trap | knob

finger | brush

paper

day

door

paint

lady		seed
hair		stand
ten		elope
mad		bush

bird

band

ant

am

hand		link
hand		how
look		side
sea		ways

cuff

some

out

side

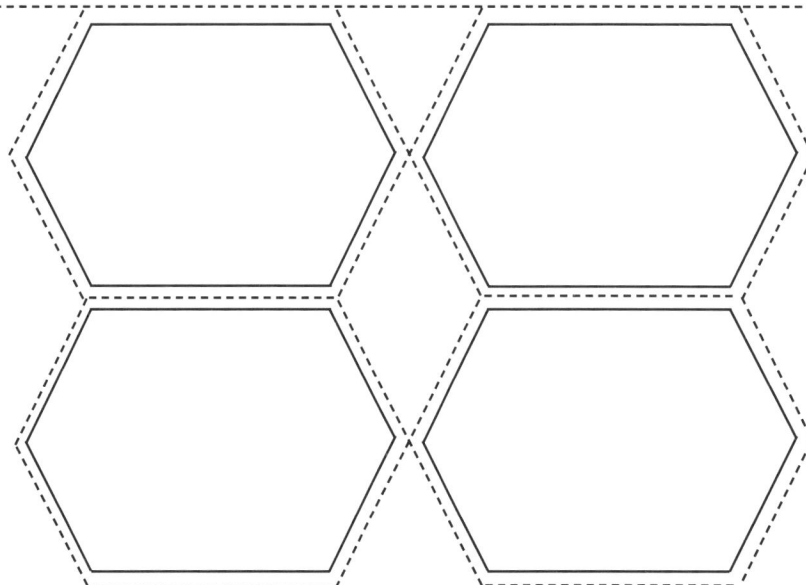

What is it?

51

Aim: The object of the game is to name different parts of a whole. Some people have difficulties which may be due to weak vocabulary development or to poor storage of these words in the brain which impairs the retrieval of the words quickly and easily.

Materials: Photocopy pages 52 - 55 onto card and cut along the dotted lines. Laminate if possible.

Game: Players work in pairs. They take it in turns to turn over a picture without letting their partner see it. They then have to name the different parts of the object so that their partner can guess what it is. Encourage the players to name parts only and not the function or use of the object,
i.e. *it has wheels, chain, saddle and handlebars* and **NOT** it is something you ride.

A page of blank cards has been included on page 56 so that more items can be added as required.

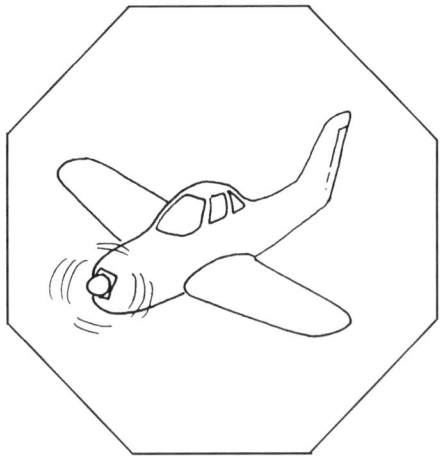

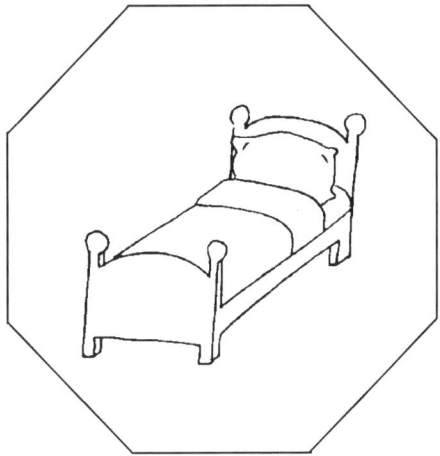

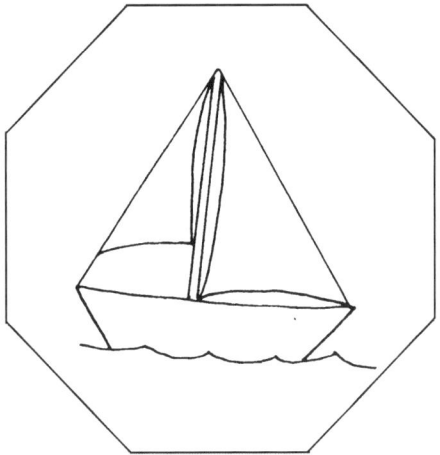
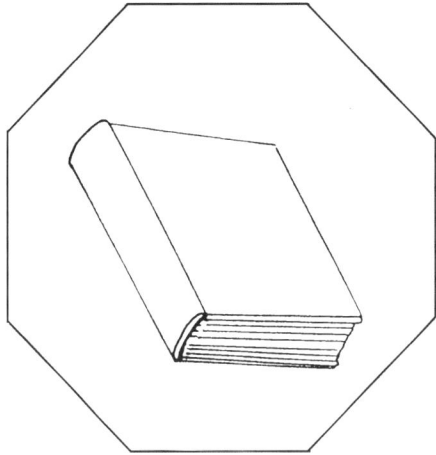
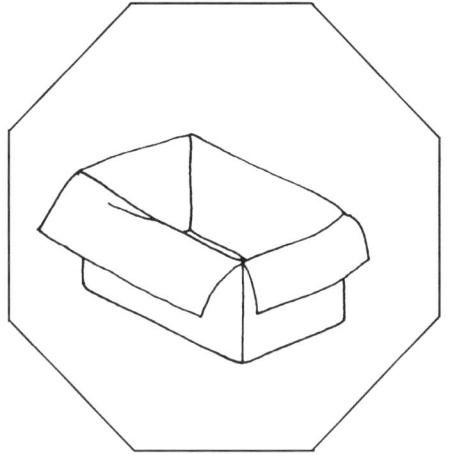
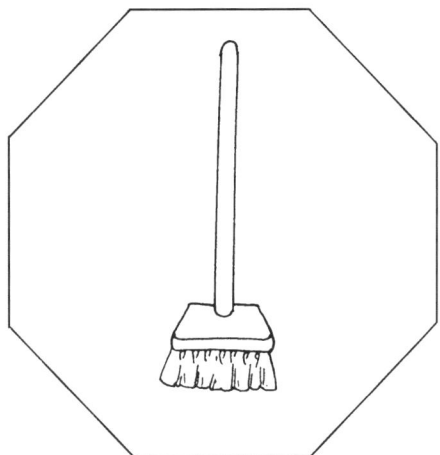

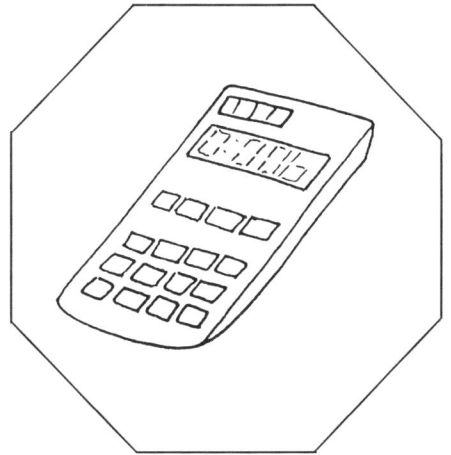

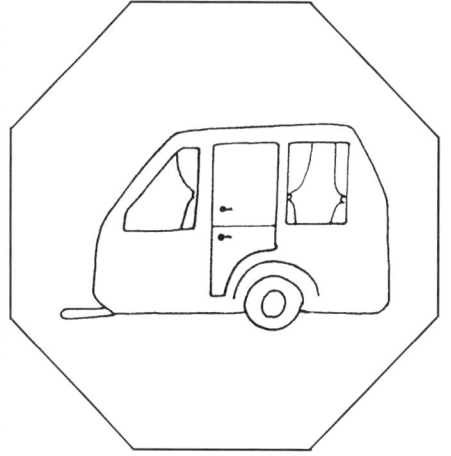
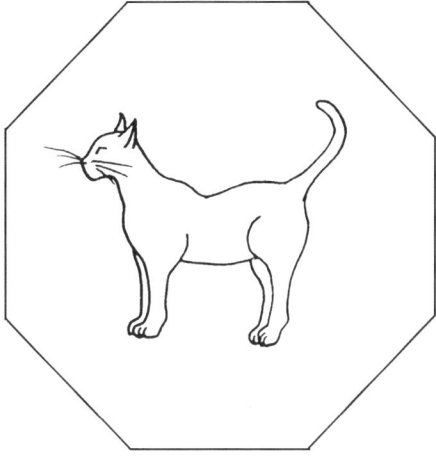
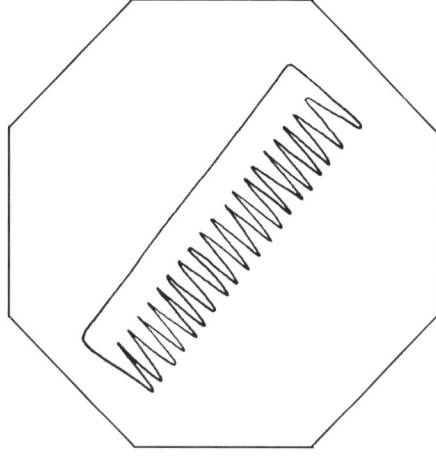
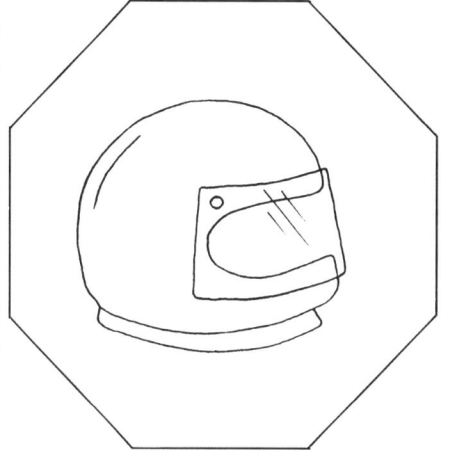
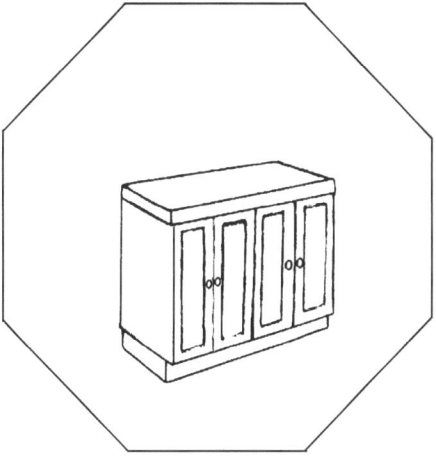

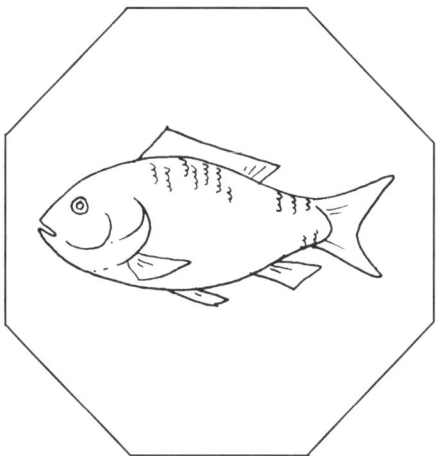

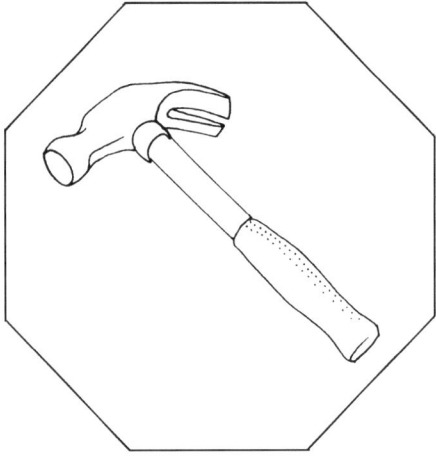

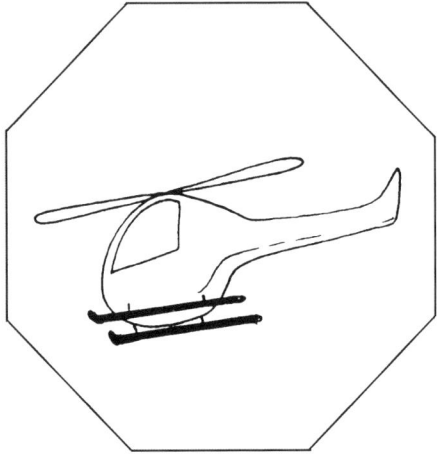

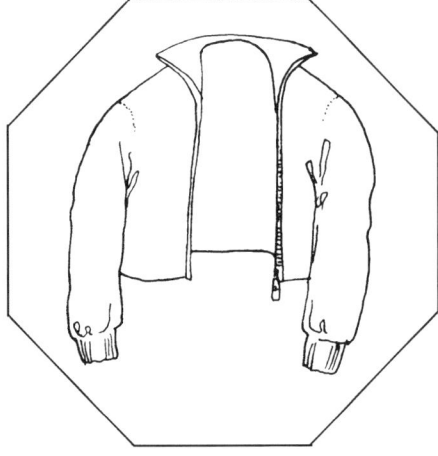
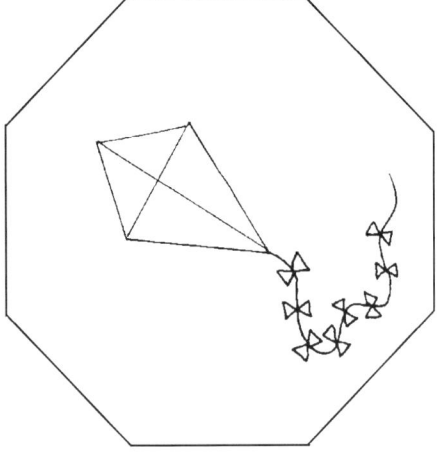
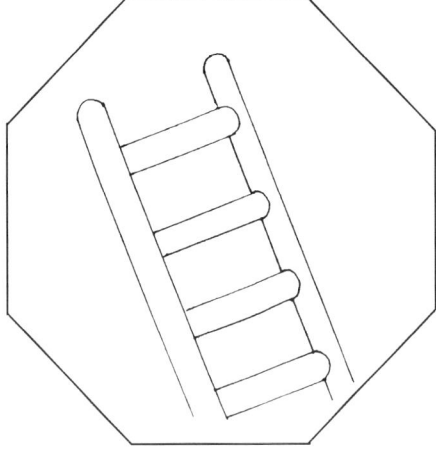
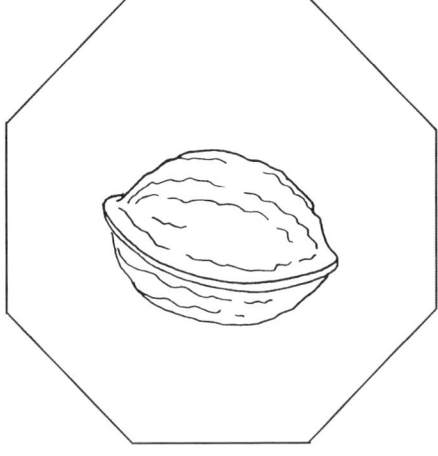
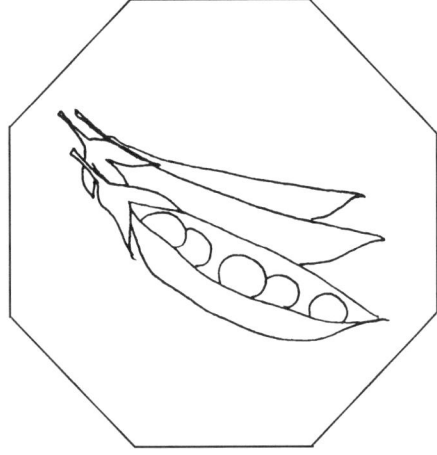
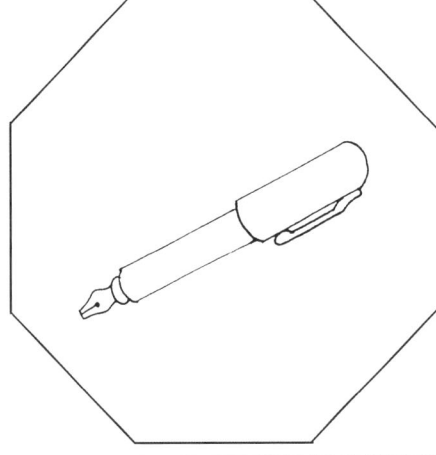
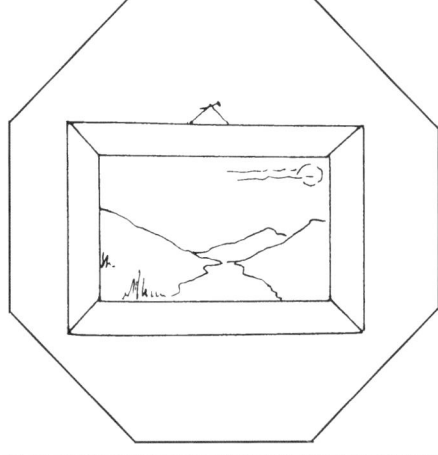

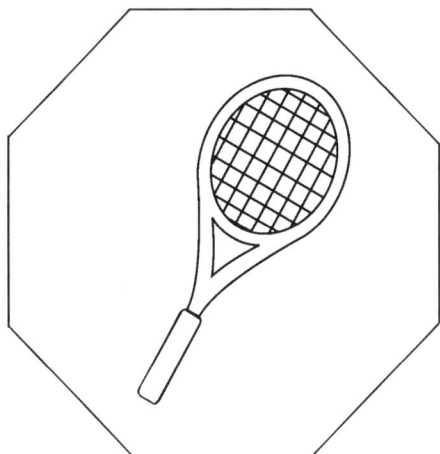

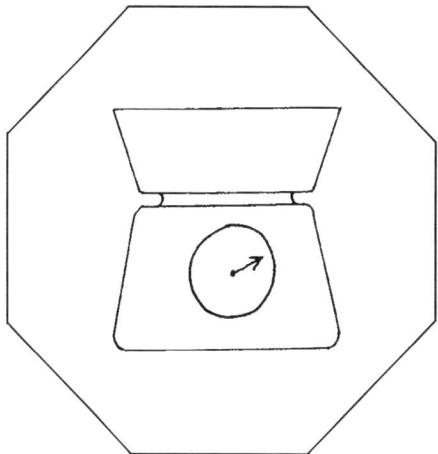

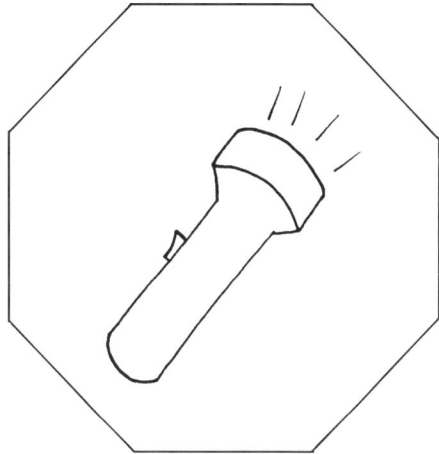

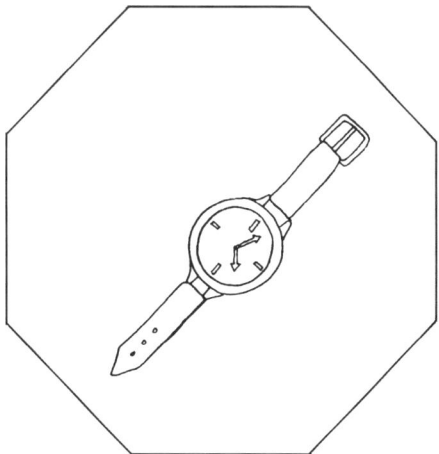
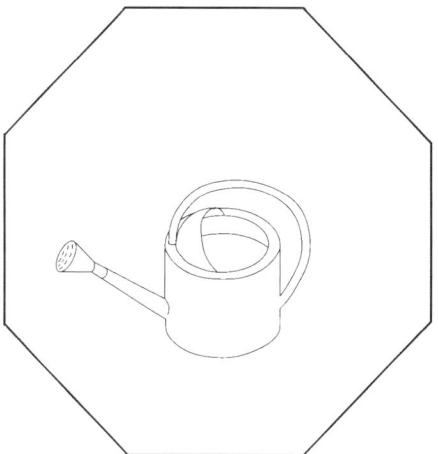
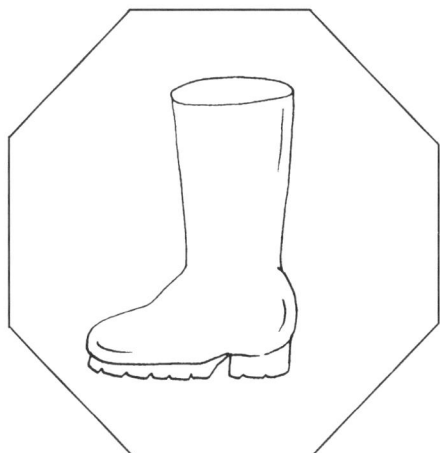
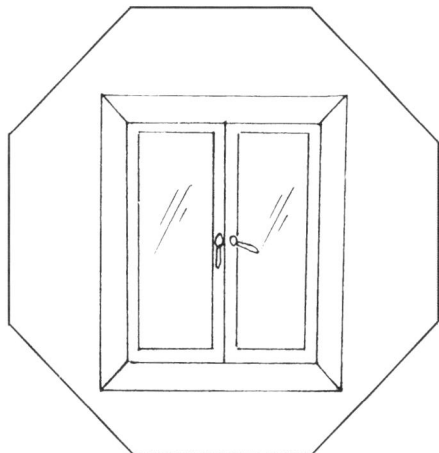
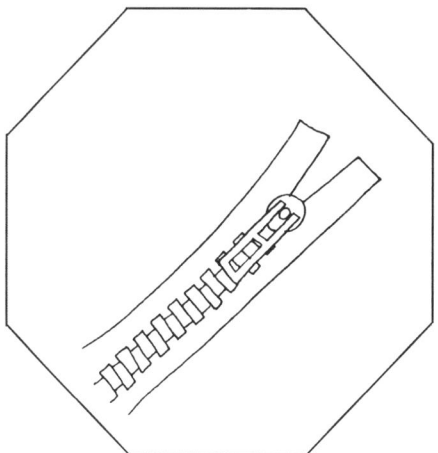

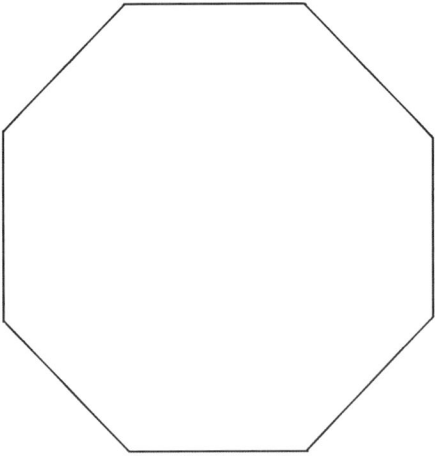
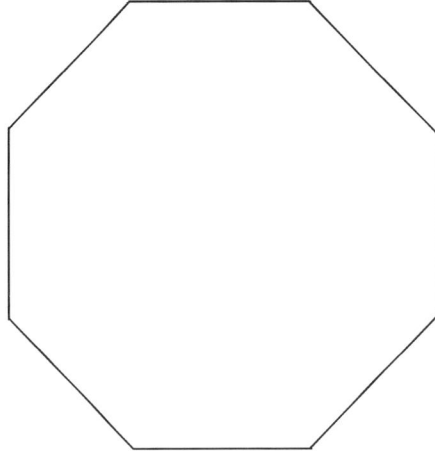
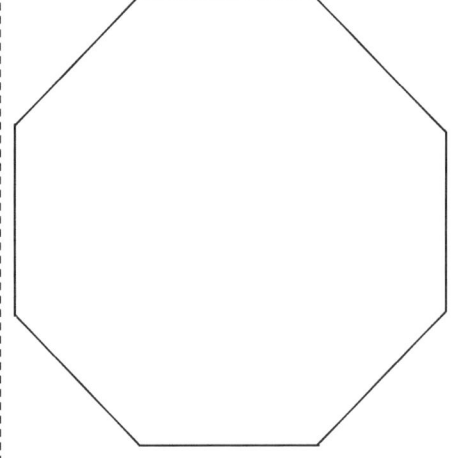
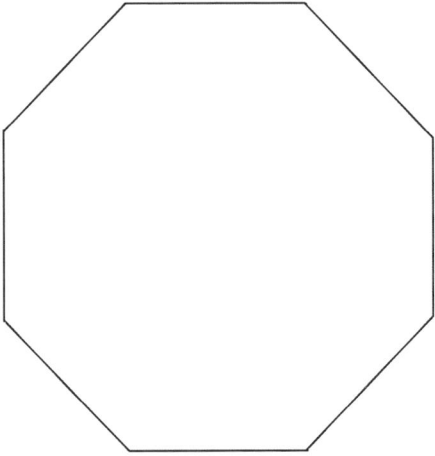
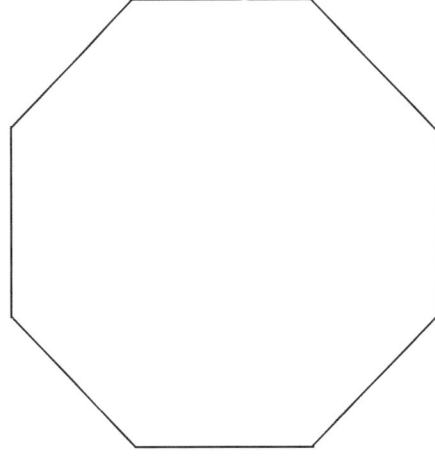
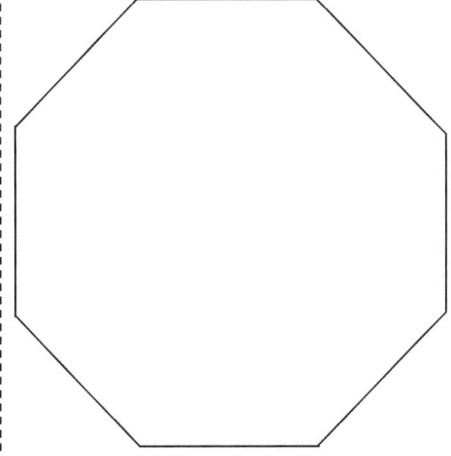
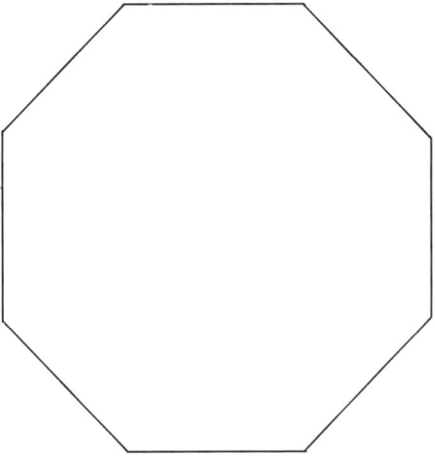
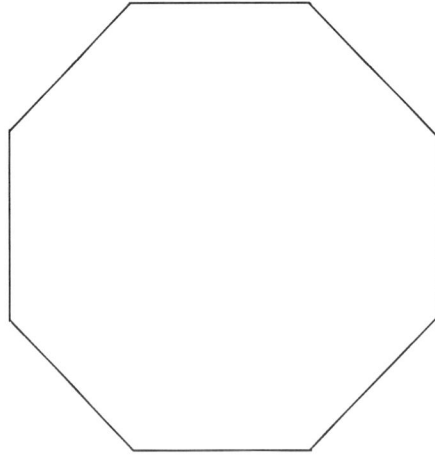
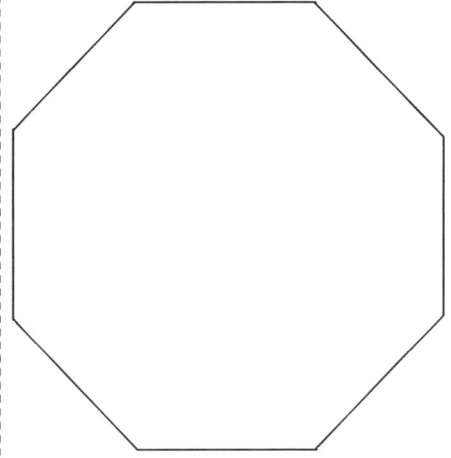
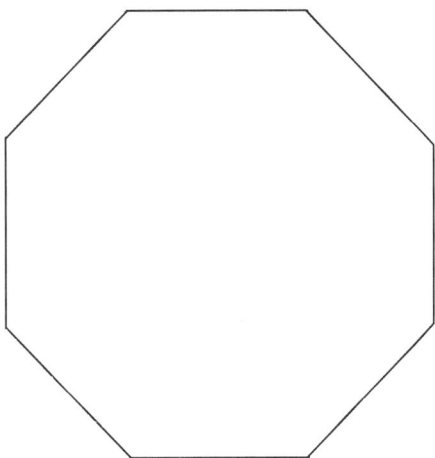
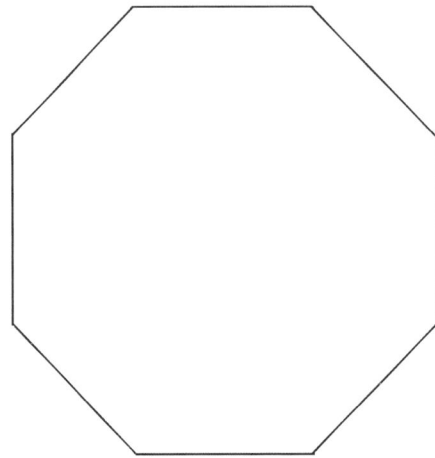
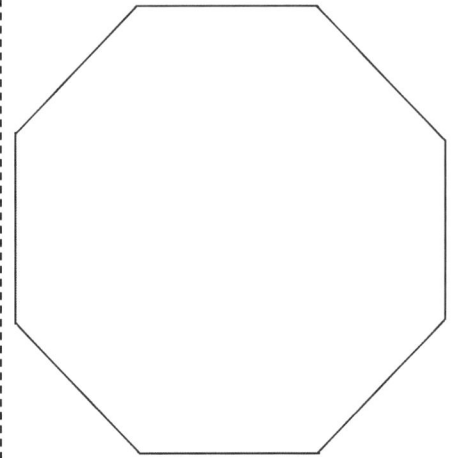

Syllables

Aim: The object of the game is to practise counting the number of syllables in multisyllabic words.

Materials: Photocopy the pictures on pages 59 - 64, onto card and cut along the dotted lines. Laminate if possible. Photocopy the game board on page 58 for each player.

Game: Shuffle the cards and place them face down in a pile on the table. Give each player a game board. Players take it in turns to take a card, say what the picture represents and how many syllables are in the word. Initially encourage players to clap or tap out the number of syllables as they say them. Players can then move a counter up one leaf of the ladybirds' beanstalks according to the number of syllables in the word. Later it is possible to move towards players internalising their counting and moving a counter round one of the game boards.

2 syllables		3 Syllables		4 Syllables	
anchor	monkey	alphabet	paper clip	alligator	operation
apple	mushroom	broccoli	pineapple	America	parking meter
bottle	pumpkin	butterfly	protractor	binoculars	photographer
camel	rabbit	caravan	rocking horse	calculator	radiator
carrots	razor	coat hanger	sandcastles	centimetre	rhinoceros
candle	ruler	daffodil	screwdriver	caterpillar	roller coaster
cupboard	scissors	dominoes	tambourine	cauliflower	sewing machine
dustpan	skate board	hamburger	triangle	certificate	television
football	teapot	computer	twenty five	exclamation	thermometer
glasses	tiger	kangaroo	umbrella	extinguisher	watering can
hammer	toaster	octopus	video	helicopter	washing machine
letter	trolley	newspaper	volcano	gladiator	wellington boot

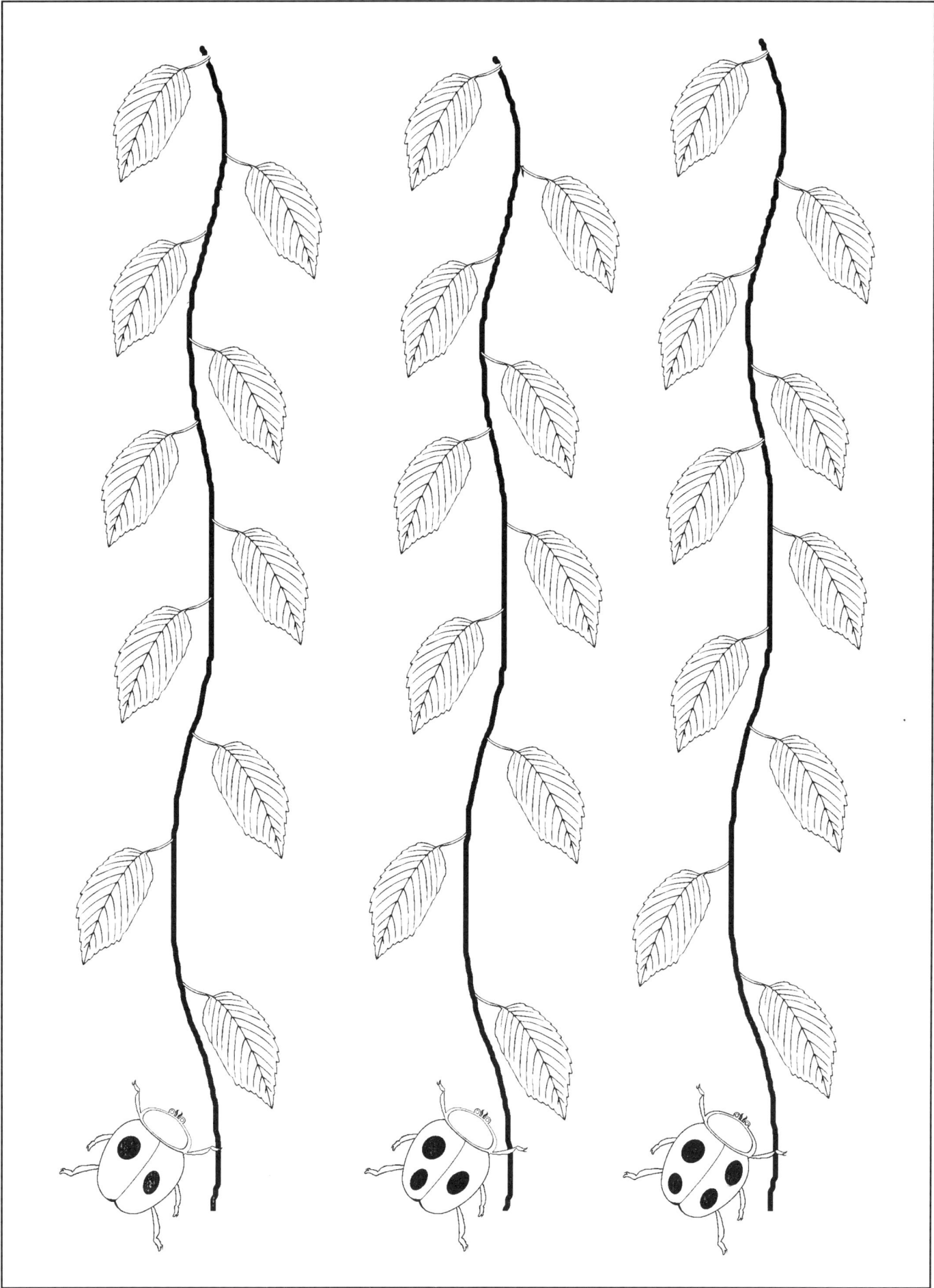

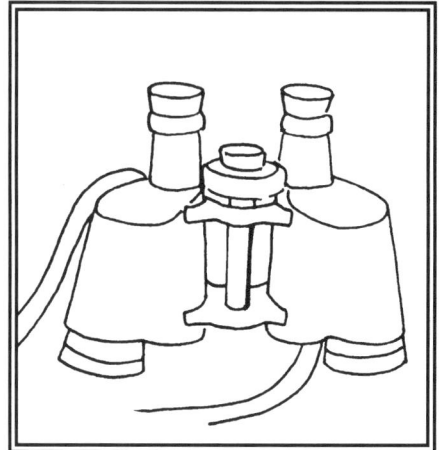

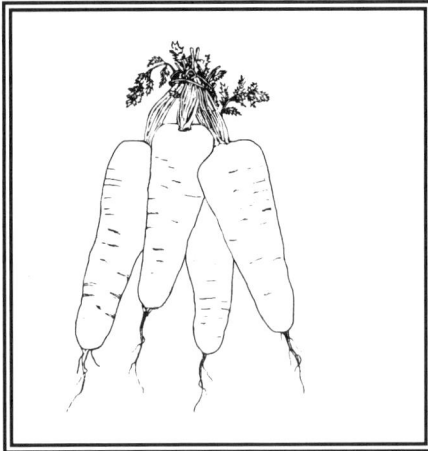

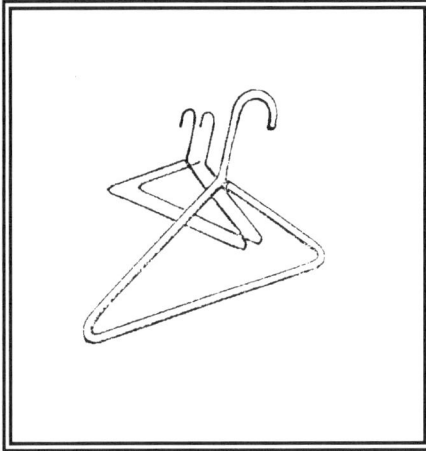

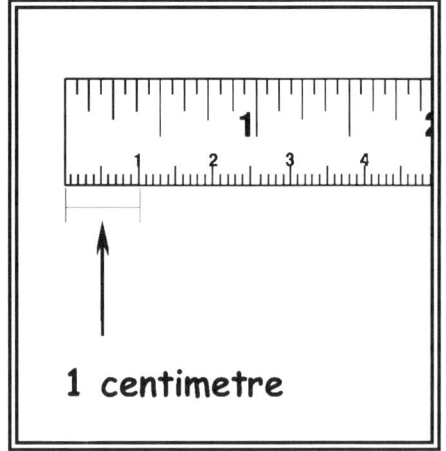

1 centimetre

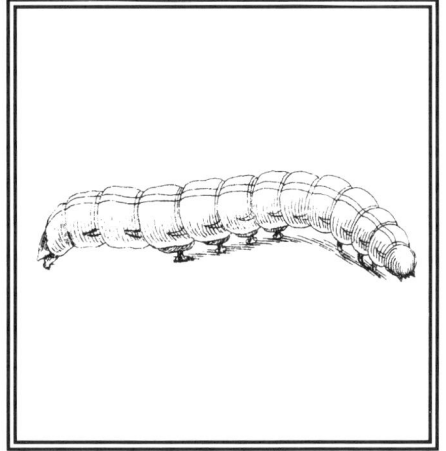

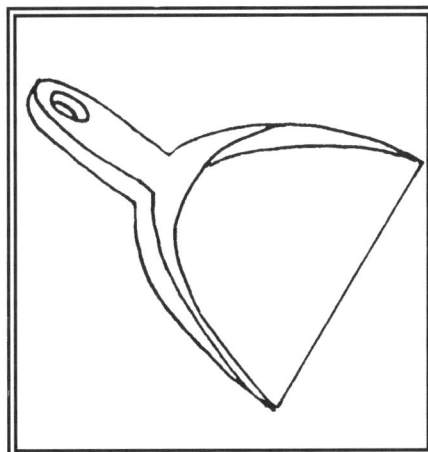

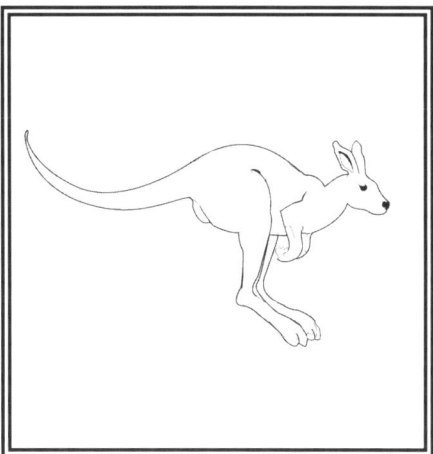
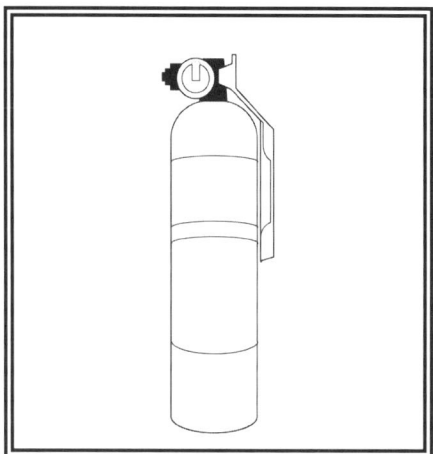
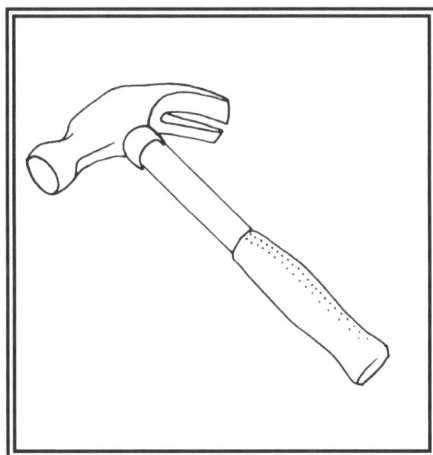

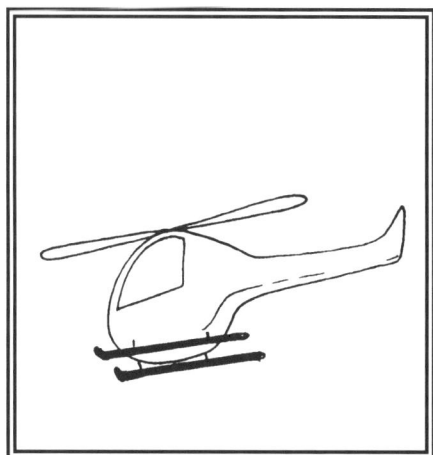

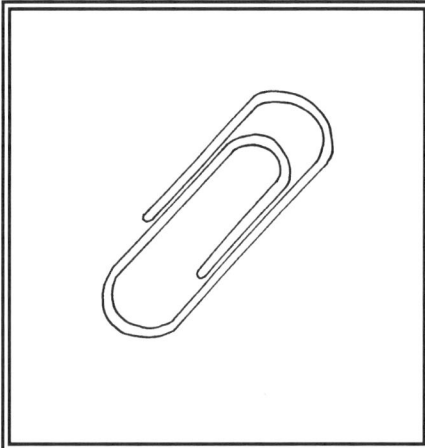
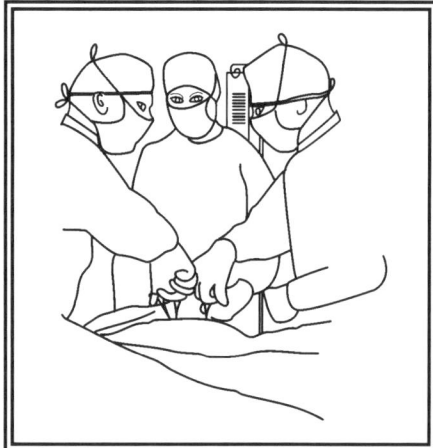
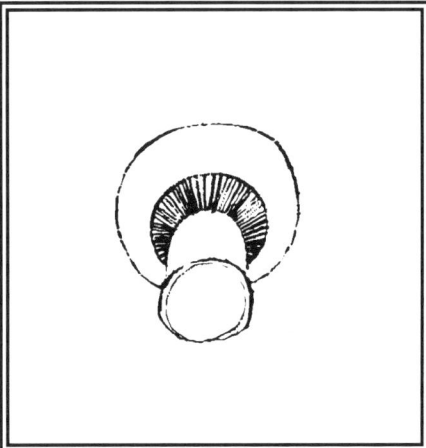

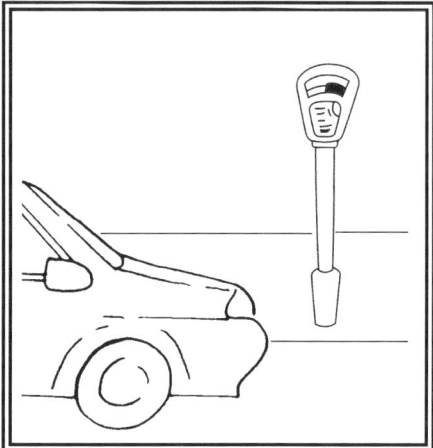

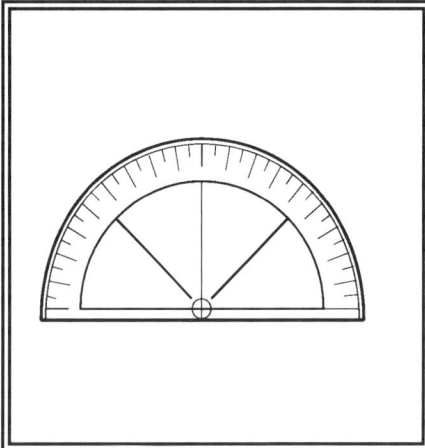

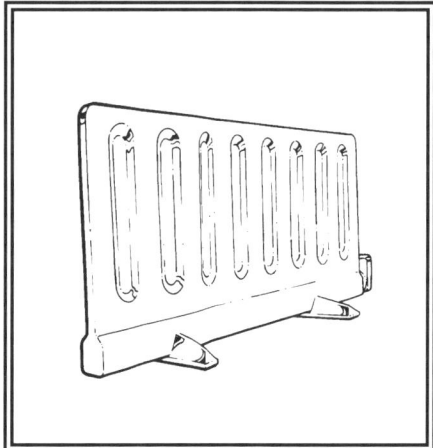

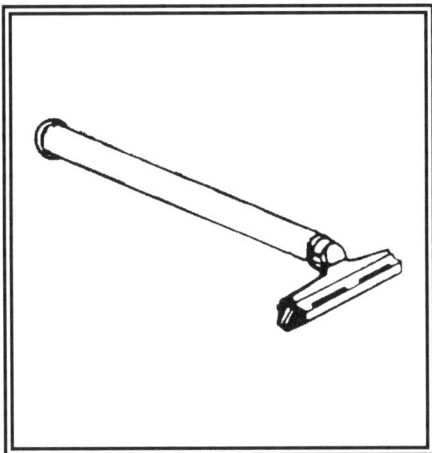

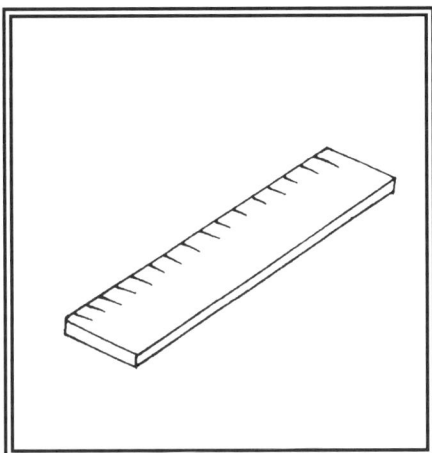
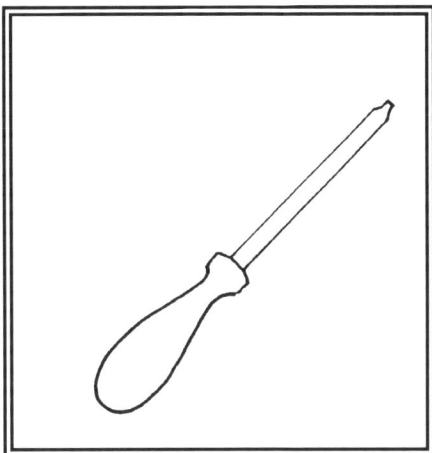

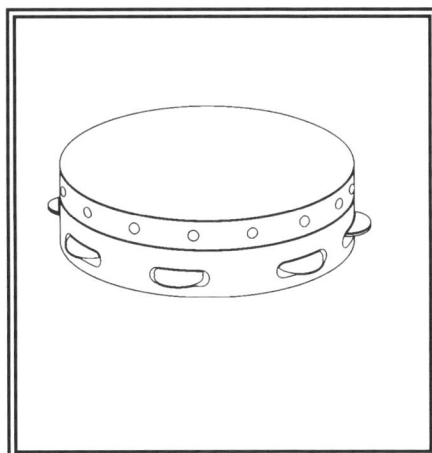
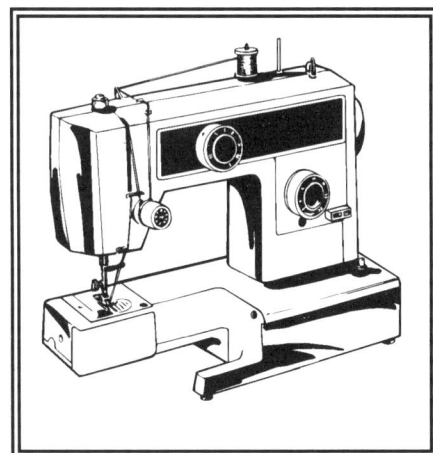
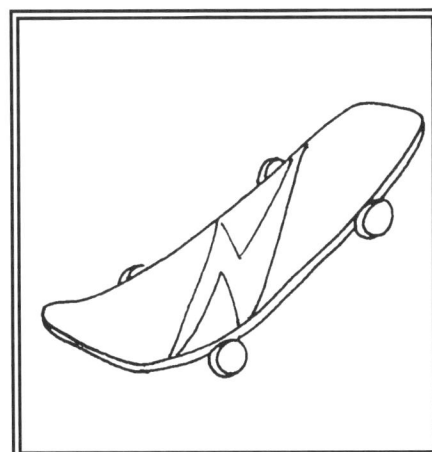
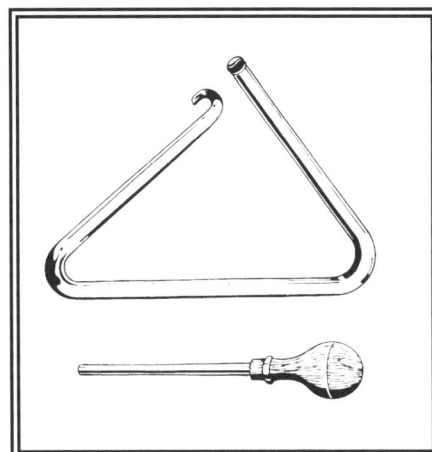

25

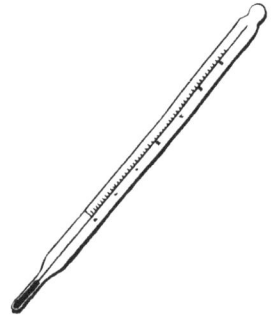

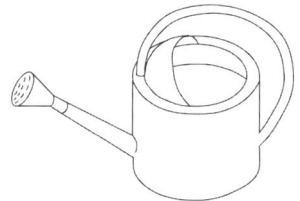

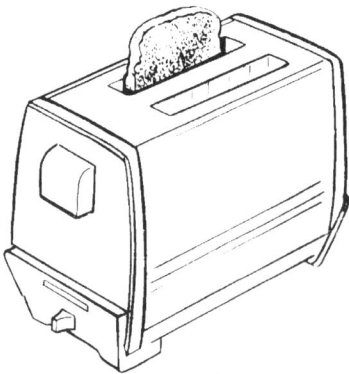

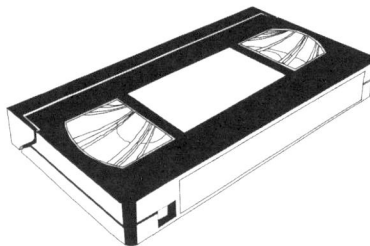

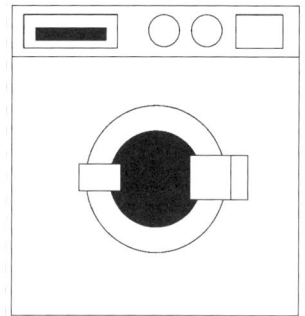

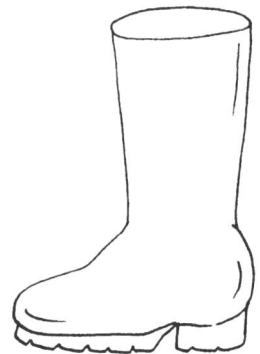

Verb Variety

65

Aim: The object of the game is to help children to suggest different verbs which will fit in a sentence.

Materials: A dice.
Photocopy pages 67 - 69 onto card and cut along the dotted lines. Laminate if possible.

Game: Place the cards in a pile face down on the table. The players take turns to turn over a card and throw the dice. The number on the dice indicates the number of different verbs they have to suggest which will fit into the sentence. Players should be encouraged to provide a variety of verbs and to be as imaginative as possible. A list of suggested verbs is given on page 66 but these should only be used as a starting point.

A page of blank cards has been included on page 70 so that additional items can be added as required.

Some suggested verbs:

1. loaded	parked	crashed	drove	polished	fixed
2. read	opened	finished	folded	bought	delivered
3. drank	made	poured	served	enjoyed	brewed
4. caught	fed	cooked	netted	weighed	gutted
5. wore	sewed	mended	ironed	tore	washed
6. folded	washed	ironed	bleached	mended	dried
7. tied	brushed	polished	wore	liked	hated
8. made	mixed	cooked	cut	tasted	sold
9. cooked	burnt	barbecued	wolfed	bought	enjoyed
10. entered	passed	searched	left	recommended	found
11. stirred	served	made	poured	burnt	heated
12. prepared	hurried	skipped	cooked	shared	began
13. saw	chased	netted	found	recognised	released
14. cleaned	lit	opened	heated	filled	closed
15. planned	booked	remembered	described	enjoyed	interrupted
16. saw	admired	loved	sketched	photographed	enjoyed
17. mended	oiled	rode	raced	mounted	sold
18. baked	kneaded	sliced	toasted	cut	buttered
19. read	posted	treasured	folded	received	kept
20. delivered	spilt	warmed	drank	collected	poured
21. carried	dressed	washed	fed	adored	cuddled
22. cleaned	tidied	closed	built	organised	filled
23. set	heard	raised	sounded	dreaded	rang
24. laid	cleaned	wiped	set	covered	polished
25. took	developed	displayed	sold	showed	kept
26. rowed	moored	capsized	sank	sailed	boarded
27. excercised	fed	groomed	collared	chased	kept
28. visited	built	bought	cleaned	explored	tidied
29. tasted	stirred	served	ladled	shared	warmed
30. opened	filled	fetched	carried	closed	gave
31. climbed	held	placed	fetched	needed	found
32. paddled	swam	sailed	fished	played	splashed
33. broke	filled	fetched	washed	admired	loved
34. swept	cleared	followed	took	found	laid
35. wound	dropped	saw	heard	mended	set
36. cut	permed	washed	styled	coloured	bleached

1. They ...... the van.

2. He ...... the newspaper.

3. Mary ...... the tea.

4. She ...... the fish.

5. Ann ...... her new dress.

6. Mum ...... the sheets.

7. Sally ...... her shoes.

8. Granny ...... a cake.

9. The scouts ...... some sausages.

10. I ...... the shop.

11. Mum ...... the custard.

12. Jack ...... his breakfast.

13 John ...... the butterfly.

14 I ...... the oven.

15 We ...... our holiday.

16 We ...... the view.

17 Fred ...... his bike.

18 Wendy ...... some bread.

19 She ...... the letter.

20 The boy ...... the milk.

21 She ...... the baby.

22 He ...... the cupboard.

23 They ...... the alarm.

24 Sam ...... the table.

25

Mel ...... the photos.

26

The children ...... the boat.

27

We ...... the dog.

28

They ...... the new house.

29

Tom ...... the soup.

30

Sally ...... the box.

31

Joe ...... the ladder.

32

They ...... in the sea.

33

Mum ...... the glass vase.

34

The boy ...... the path.

35

The girl ...... the clock.

36

The hairdresser ...... her hair.

Tricky Tenses

Aim: The object of the game is to practise using the past, present and future forms of verbs. 60 verbs with irregular past tenses have been illustrated.

Materials: A dice.
A counter for each player.
Photocopy pages 73 - 77 onto card and cut along the dotted lines. Laminate if possible.
Photocopy the board on page 72.

Game: Place the cards face down on the table. Players take it in turns to turn over a card and decide on the verb to be used. They throw the dice and move their counter round the board - in any direction. The square they land on gives them the start of a sentence to use with their verb,
e.g. Yesterday he hit the ball.
      Today he is hitting the ball
      Next Friday he will hit the ball
Encourage the use of full sentences.
Players can keep their own score of the number of points they win by answering correctly.

A page of blank cards has been included on page 78 so that additional items can be added.

Verbs illustrated:

bend	blow	break	build	burn	burst
buy	catch	choose	cut	dig	do
draw	drink	drive	eat	fall	feed
fight	fly	get	give	grow	hang
has/hold	hide	hit	is	kneel	lie
light	put	read	ride	ring	run
see	sell	send	shake	shoot	shut
sing	sink	sit	sleep	spill	spin
spread	stand	steal	sweep	swim	take
tear	think	throw	wear	win	write

at eight o'clock **10**

6 last night

3 this morning

2 tomorrow

3 this evening

2 on weekdays

5 a month ago

6 next Friday

4 this month

at present **2**

2 up to now

an hour ago **2**

4 last Sunday

3 today

next month **2**

1 tonight

soon **1**

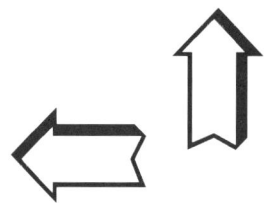

just now **2**

6 yesterday

2 on holiday

last week **5**

4 later on

earlier **10**

START

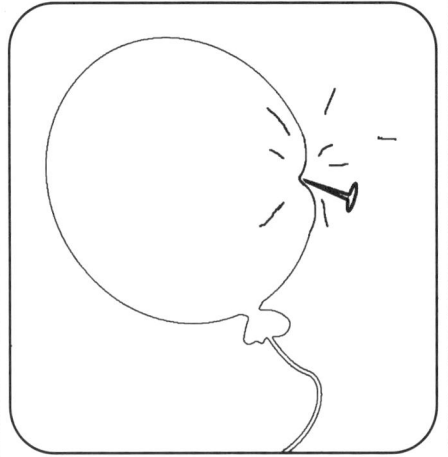

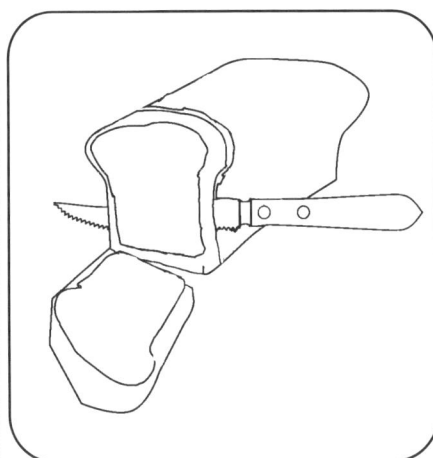

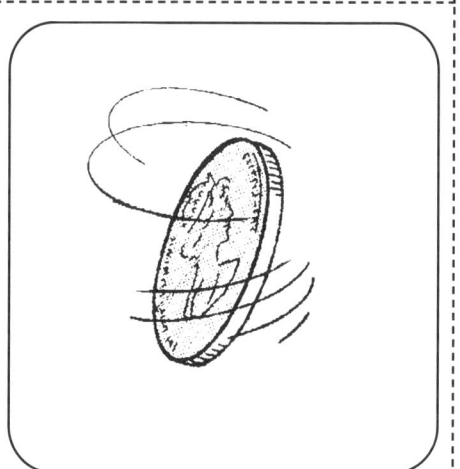

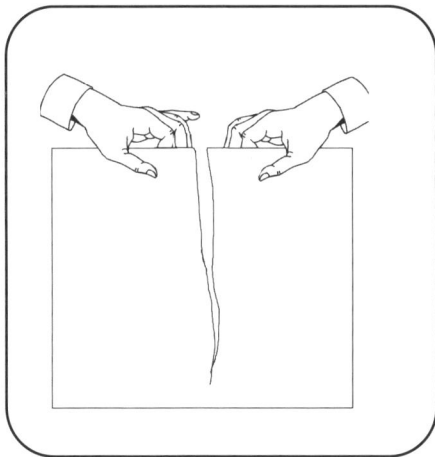

Adding Adjectives

Aim: The object of the game is to supply a variety of adjectives to go with a noun and put them in the right order in a phrase.

Materials: Photocopy pages 80 - 87 onto card and cut along the dotted lines. Laminate if possible.

Game: Give each player 4 - 6 adjective strips to place in front of them. Put the adjective cards face down in a pile on the table. Players take it in turns to turn over a card and read out the adjective on it. If the player can use the adjective, he keeps it but if not he calls Who wants it? and the first player to respond gets it. If a players calls for a card but cannot use it, he misses a turn and the adjective is placed at the bottom of the pile.
Once all the adjectives have been shared out, players must try to put 3 adjectives on their adjective lines to make sense.

A page of blank cards has been included on page 88 so that additional items can be added.

blue	plastic	toy
old	dirty	brown
friendly	soft	furry
rusty	old	slow
beautiful	large	purple
bright	shiny	red

tasty	ripe	yellow
long	strong	wooden
fast	wooden	new
cosy	green	canvas
leaky	broken	fountain
tall	leafy	shady

frisky	brown	friendly
fresh	crisp	juicy
favourite	warm	woolly
new	exciting	mystery
scruffy	worn	blue
loveable	obedient	family

small	wooden	sailing
round	rubber	bouncy
big	red	plastic
fierce	wild	hungry
hard	wooden	kitchen
sweet	red	ripe

Alternative Adjectives

Aim: The object of the game is to supply a variety of
                adjectives to go with a picture of a noun.

Materials: Photocopy the pictures from pages 90 - 93 onto card
                and cut along the dotted lines. Laminate if possible.
                A spinner.

Game: Put the picture cards face down in a pile on the table.
                Players take it in turns to turn over a picture card and
                spin the spinner. They then have to give the number of
                adjectives as shown by the spinner (1 - 4) which would
                describe the picture. Encourage them to put the adjectives
                in a sentence,
                i.e. I saw a *colourful* butterfly
                    I saw a *small, colourful* butterfly
                    She slept in a *comfortable* bed
                    She slept in a *large, comfortable* bed
                    She slept in a *new, large, comfortable, wooden* bed

This game can be played in conjunction with one of the board games at
the end of the book.

A page of blank cards has been included on page 94 so that additional
items can be added.

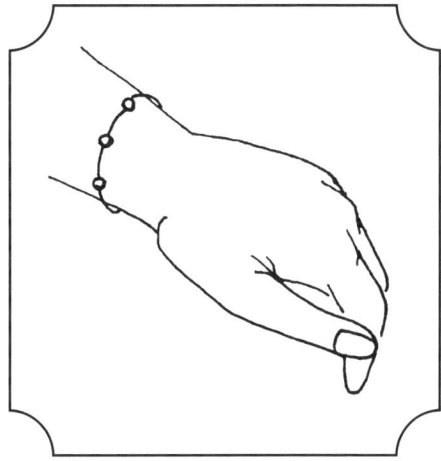

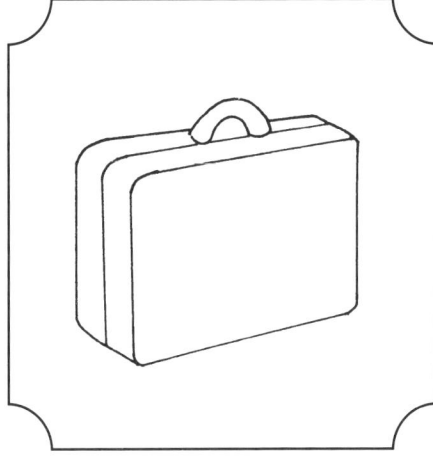

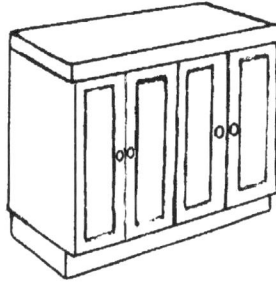

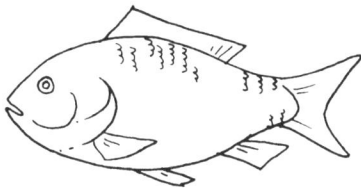

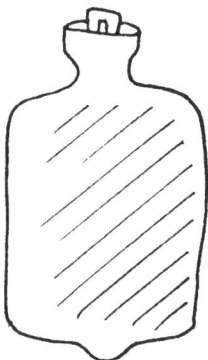

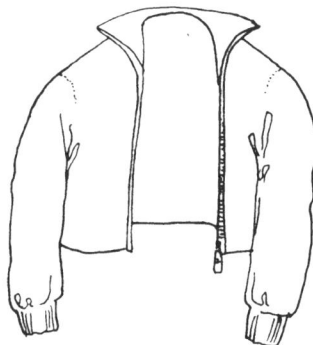

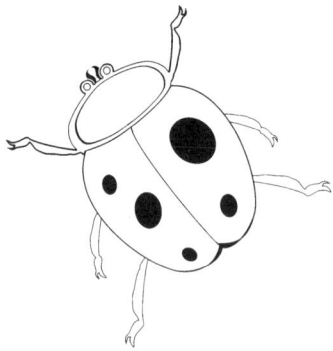

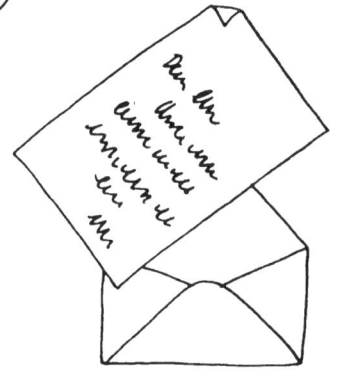

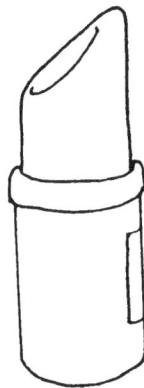

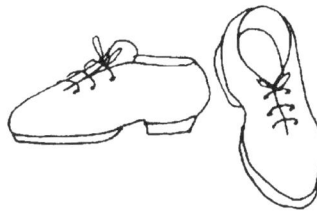

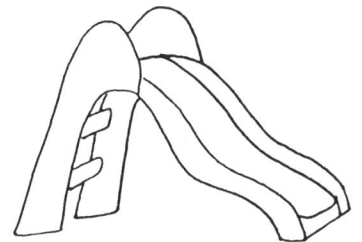

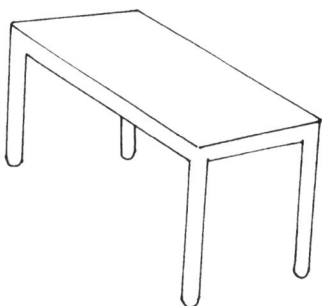

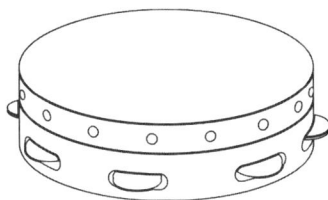

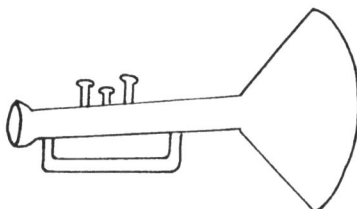

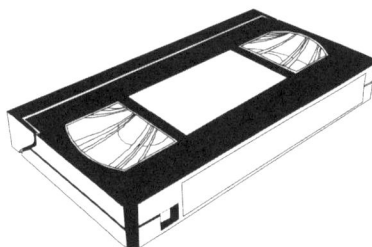

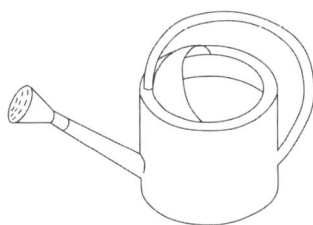

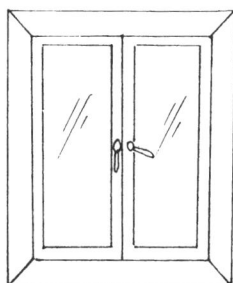

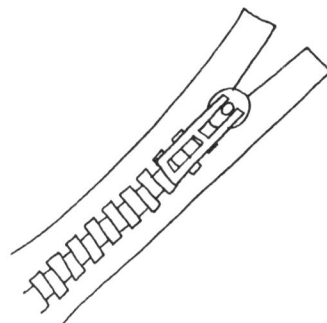

Clever Conjunctions

Aim: The object of the game is to practise the use of conjunctions and to produce a phrase to complete a sentence.

Materials: Photocopy pages 97 - 99 onto card and cut along the dotted lines. Laminate if possible.
Photocopy page 96 and cut into 2 halves.
A dice.

Game: Place the sentence cards face down in a pile on the table. Select either the first or second half of page 96 and display it. Players take it in turns to throw the dice to select a conjunction and then to pick a sentence card and complete the sentence using that conjunction.

A page of blank cards has been included on page 100 so that additional items can be added.

and

but

because

although

so

when

since

then

before

after

while

as

The first girl wore a new dress...

She blushed bright red...

The front door flew open...

The hairdresser closed the shop...

The street lamp fell over...

The blue jacket hung in the wardrobe...

All the lights went out...

My ginger cat gets frightened...

The girl ran to the park...

My watch needs a new battery...

The circus came last Summer...

The school bus hit the wall...

New shoes can be uncomfortable...

The black dog hurt his paw...

The old man was angry...

There was an almighty crash...

She laughed out loud ...

Joe slammed the door...

Lizzie put on her boots ...

The teacher opened the book...

The boy felt very guilty...

Mum put the kettle on...

The dog barked at the door...

The sky clouded over...

The friends got on the bus...	Tim opened the box ...
The football coach blew his whistle...	The man bought her some flowers...
They all sat down at the table...	He dug a hole...
Two of them went to the cinema...	John washed the car...
They clapped their hands...	The ball went into the water...
Jane waited patiently ...	They rushed to the hospital ...

Adventurous Adverbs

Aim: The object of the game is to illustrate the use of adverbs.

Materials: Photocopy the verb pictures on pages 73 - 77 and the adverbs on pages 102 - 103 onto card and cut along the dotted lines. Laminate if possible.

Game: Lay out 6 verb pictures and a variety of adverbs. Each player takes it in turn to pick a verb picture and find 2 or more different adverbs which could be used with the verb. Encourage the use of full sentences, e.g. The man is drinking thirstily, or the man is drinking slowly.

A page of blank cards has included on page 104 so that additional items can be added as required.

sometimes	now	here
still	soon	there
usually	later	outside
always	hourly	inside
often	yesterday	upstairs
never	today	away
early	tomorrow	abroad
late	daily	somewhere

slowly	kindly	noisily
painfully	stupidly	badly
softly	loudly	greedily
forcefully	reluctantly	hungrily
accidentally	happily	heavily
carefully	excitedly	fiercely
skillfully	quickly	generously
cleverly	thirstily	unexpectedly

When, Where, How?

105

Aim: The object of the game is to illustrate the use of a
                  variety of kinds of adverbs in a sentence.

Materials: Photocopy the verb pictures on pages 73 - 77.
                  Photocopy the adverbs on pages 102 - 103 and page 106.

Game: Place page 106 on the table with the questions When,
                  Where and How? Each player takes it in turn to pick a
                  verb picture to make a sentence using the verb together
                  with adverbs of time, place and manner.
                  e.g. **Yesterday** the boy **carefully** drew a picture **here**.
                  The adverb cards can be used as a prompt. Adverbial
                  phrases can be introduced, e.g. at home, last night, etc.

When

Where

How

Silly Sentences

Aim: The object of the game is to illustrate the use of pronouns by using them instead of nouns in a sentence.

Materials: Photocopy pages 108 - 109 onto card and cut along the dotted lines. Laminate if possible.

Game: Shuffle the cards and place face down in the centre of the table. Players take it in turns to take a card and read it aloud (help may be given as required). Discuss the fact that the sentences sound silly due to the repetition and redundancy of nouns. Players are then encouraged to repeat the sentence and make it sound better by replacing nouns with pronouns where appropriate.

This can be used in conjunction with one of the board games at the end of the book.

A page of blank cards has been included on page 110 so that additional items can be added as required.

John took Mary's dog for a walk to John's friend's house.

Bill told Bill's friend that Bill was going out.

Helen went to Mary and Helen's school.

Mum said "Mum and Joe are going to the Park."

Sally's teacher told Sally that Sally had done well.

The girl said that the man told the boy and the girl to go away.

Bill and Mary both got watches for Bill and Mary's birthdays.

Mary and Joan said, "Can Mary and Joan have Mary and Joan's tea?"

The dog hurt the dog's paw on the path.

Mum said, "Mum wants Peter and Jim to come for tea."

Tom said, "The day was sunny and Bob and Tom went away."

Joe said, "Joe and Tim took Joe and Tim's cat to the vet."

Joan said, "Joan's Mum said Joan could have the treat."

Harry washed Harry in the bath.

Leo said, "Can Leo go to Leo's room?"

Mum said, "Mum's finger is sore."

Don hurt Don when Don fell.

The two girls took the two girl's bikes for a ride on Jean's birthday.

Sally said, "Where can Sally get Sally a haircut?

"The boy is tired so find another boy to play with," the boy said.

John said," The book is John's."

The girl found that the bird had built the bird's nest in the girl's garden.

Mum said, "Jean tries to make Jean popular."

"Put the item Mum is holding in Mum's bag," Mum said to John.

Sillier Sentences

Aim: The object of the game is to illustrate the appropriate use of nouns and pronouns in a sentence.

Materials: Photocopy pages 112 - 113 onto card and cut along the dotted lines. Laminate if possible.

Game: Shuffle the cards and place face down in the centre of the table. Players take it in turns to take a card and read it aloud (help may be given as required). Discuss the fact that the meaning of the sentences is hard to understand out of context. Players are then encouraged to repeat the sentence and make it clearer by replacing pronouns with nouns where appropriate. Different members of the group could suggest different nouns to change the meaning of the sentence.

This can be used in conjunction with one of the board games at the end of the book.

A page of blank cards has been included on page 114 so that additional items can be added as required.

He said he was going to give it to him.

She told him they had run away.

"You will find it in her kitchen", she said.

She went with her to see it.

She took his car to visit her.

They went to their party when they found it.

She went on holiday with her in her new car.

He took it for a walk with him and her to their house.

He called 999 and he came to rescue him from it.

You and I are going somewhere.

He told them to pick it up.

Everyone come and see this.

Put it in there for them and don't tell them about it.

Something happened when he went to see that.

He has to go if they tell him to.

She said she could not do it for them.

He was cross with him for missing it.

She made herself do it for their sake.

Carry this over there and put it in that, please.

Put it in their thing for me.

You told her about that when she asked about it.

They were pleased with them when they passed.

He loves to go there when he has that.

Tell her about it when you see them.

Multiple Meanings

Aim: To give several meanings of one word.

Materials: Photocopy pages 116 - 119 onto card and cut along the dotted lines. Laminate if possible.

Game: Shuffle the cards and place in a pile face down on the table. Players take it in turns to turn over a card and read the word out loud. They then have to think of as many different meanings as they can for the word. Give help as required, e.g.

Is it a noun or naming word -
        Can you say *a......* or *the......*
Is it a verb or doing word -
        Can you say *I am ......* or *he ....*
Is it an adjective or describing word -
        Can you say *a ...... thing*

This can be played in conjunction with the ladder game on page 12, the ladybird game on page 58 or one of the board games at the back of the book.

A page of blank cards has been included on page 120 so that additional items can be added as required.

bank	bat
catch	change
check	crane
corn	down
express	face
fair	fire

fork	form
ground	hide
hit	kind
lace	lean
master	match
mean	model

odd	orange
part	pick
place	plane
point	press
right	rock
root	saw

school	score
sock	sound
spoke	spring
square	stick
stamp	suit
table	wave

More Meanings

Aim: To find one word which will fit into two sentences to illustrate different meanings.

Materials: Photocopy pages 122 - 123 onto card and cut along the dotted lines. Laminate if possible.

Game: Shuffle the cards and place in a pile face down on the table. Players take it in turns to turn over a card and read the two sentences on it (give help as required). Players then have to suggest one word which will fit into both sentences.

This can be played in conjunction with one of the board games at the back of the book.

A page of blank cards has been included on page 124 so that additional items can be added as required.

1. lock	7. row	13. watch	19. drop
2. stamp	8. swallow	14. charge	20. spot
3. book	9. calf	15. band	21. post
4. bowl	10. litter	16. pound	22. coach
5. blind	11. bark	17. dart	23. mouse
6. coat	12. train	18. shed	24. ring

1

A key is used to _____ a door.

He cut off a _____ of her hair.

7

Oars are used to _____ a boat.

I sat in the back _____ of seats.

2

She stuck a _____ on her letter.

Don't you _____ your foot at me!

8

He had to _____ his medicine.

A ___ is a bird with a forked tail.

3

He read an exciting _____.

Can I ___ a ticket for next week?

9

The cow had a baby _____.

He pulled a ___ muscle in his leg.

4

He had a _____ of soup.

It's my turn to _____ the ball.

10

The cat had a _____ of kittens.

Don't drop _____ on the beach.

5

A _____ person cannot see.

Close the _____ over the window.

11

The tree has a very rough ___ .

The dog began to ___ at the door.

6

He gave it a fresh _____ of paint.

I have a warm _____ for winter.

12

You get a _____ at the station.

The team had to ___ for the match.

13

I look at my _____ to tell the time.

We did not _____ television.

14

What does he _____ for that?

The angry bull began to _____ .

15

They danced to a _____ at the party.

He wore a _____ round his head.

16

He found a _____ coin.

He started to _____ at the door.

17

Tom threw the _____ at the board.

She saw her _____ into the shop.

18

The snake _____ its skin.

I keep tools in the garden _____.

19

She had a tear _____ on her cheek.

I tried not to _____ the cup.

20

She had a _____ on her chin.

Can you _____ the mistake?

21

Don't forget to _____ my letter.

The car hit the fence _____.

22

The team had a new_____ .

They went by _____ to the seaside.

23

You use a _____ with a computer.

A_____is an animal that eats cheese.

24

I'll _____ you next week to tell you.

He bought her a beautiful _____.

Same or Different?

Aim: To be able to say whether two words are the same or opposite in meaning

Materials: Photocopy pages 126 - 129 onto card and cut along the dotted lines. Laminate if possible.

Game: Shuffle the cards and place face down on the table. Players take it in turns to pick a card and read the two words on it (give help as required). They then have to decide whether the two words are the same or opposite in meaning. Players can be encouraged to think of other words which are the same or opposite in meaning to the words.

This can be played in conjunction with one of the games at the back of the book.

A page of blank cards has been included on page 130 so that additional items can be added as required.

bent * straight

brief * short

burn * singe

cheap * dear

cheerful * miserable

chilly * frosty

clear * opaque

clumsy * skillful

consume * eat

cross * angry

damp * moist

deep * shallow

dull ✳ shiny

easy ✳ difficult

educate ✳ teach

empty ✳ full

fail ✳ succeed

free ✳ release

friend ✳ enemy

generous ✳ selfish

hard ✳ soft

heavy ✳ weighty

hint ✳ suggest

hungry ✳ starving

junior * senior

knock * tap

lazy * idle

leap * jump

leave * depart

neglect * ignore

noise * silence

odd * even

old * antique

plentiful * sparse

powerful * strong

quick * rapid

remember * forget

rescue * save

right * left

search * find

stopper * plug

sweet * sour

talk * speak

try * attempt

war * peace

wide * narrow

yearn * long

young * old

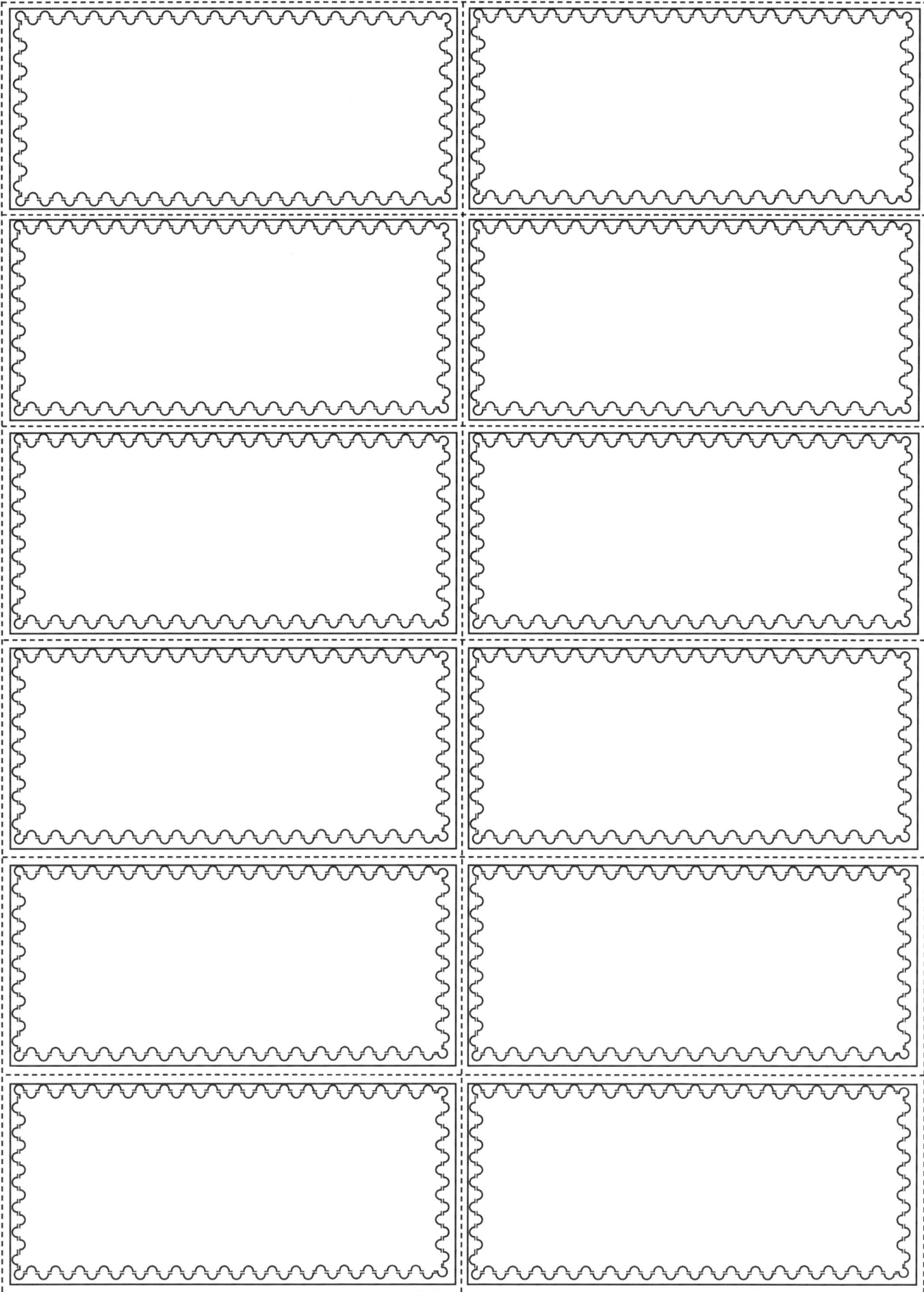

Antonyms and Synonyms

Aim: To give a word which either means the same or the opposite of a given word.

Materials: Photocopy pages 133 - 135 onto card and cut along the dotted lines. Laminate if possible.
Photocopy the board on page 132.
A dice.
A counter for each player.

Game: Players take it in turn to turn over a card and read the word on it. Players move around the board according to the number of the dice. If they land on a white square they have to give a word which means the same as the word on the card, if they land on a black square they have to give a word which means the opposite of the word on the card.

A page of blank cards has been included on page 136 so that additional items can be added as required.

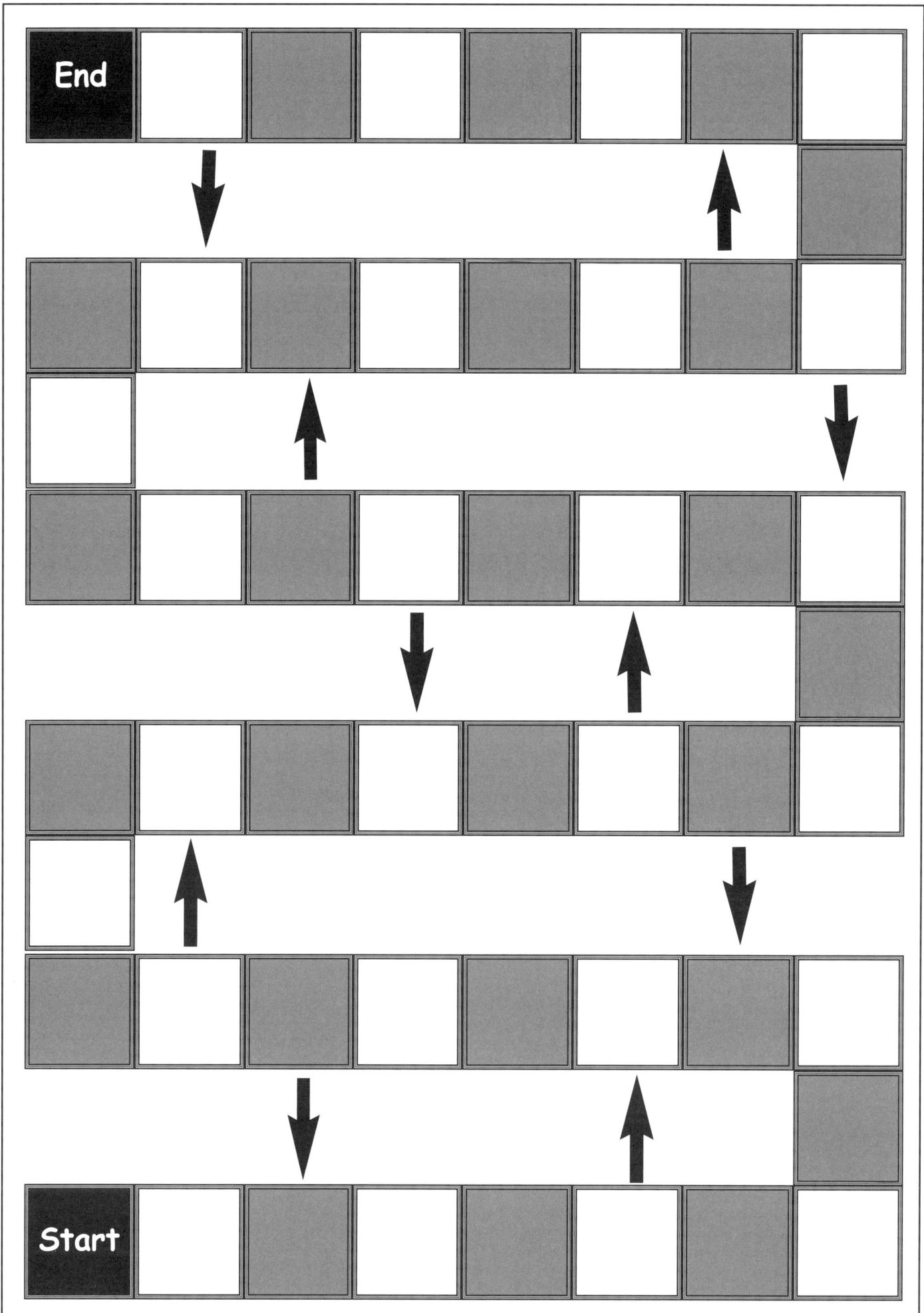

End

Start

add	bad
break	build
buy	cry
difficult	dirty
enjoy	exit
expensive	find

finish	freeze
happy	high
ill	lazy
lift	lock
lose	loud
love	pale

pull	quick
sharp	shine
shut	sink
stop	tidy
top	true
warm	wet

Antonym & Synonym Crosswords

Aim: To give a word which either means the same or the opposite of a given word.

Materials: Photocopy either the antonym crosswords on pages 138 and 139 or the synonym crosswords on pages 140 and 141.

Game: Players can either work on the crosswords individually, in pairs or in groups. Generally it is easier to think of words which are opposite in meaning than those which are the same so it is suggested that the antonym crosswords are used first. Answers are on page 142.

The answers are words which mean the opposite of the clues

Across:
1. full
4. begins
6. leaves
7. laugh
8. strong

Down:
1. difficult
2. war
3. no
5. light

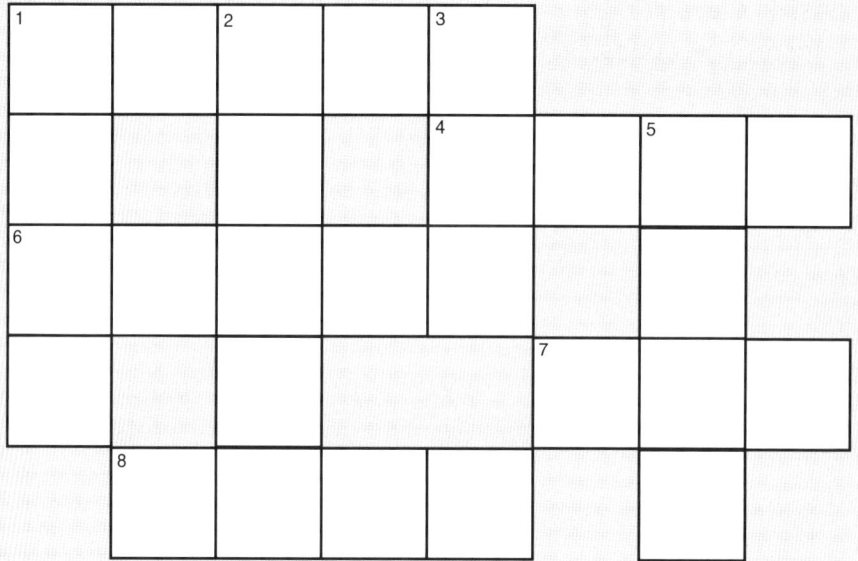

The answers are words which mean the opposite of the clues

Across:
1. clean
4. quiet
6. bad

Down:
1. bright
2. smooth
3. even
5. don't

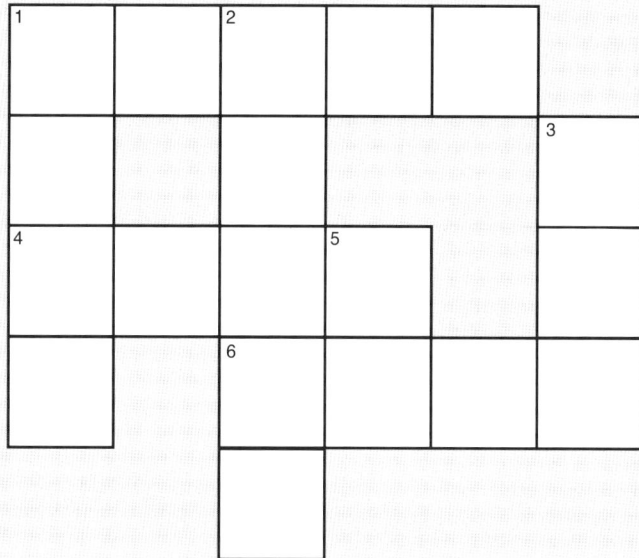

The answers are words which mean the opposite of the clues

Across:
1. new
5. over
6. late
8. fast
9. trap

Down:
1. shuts
2. sell
3. subtract
4. agree
7. high

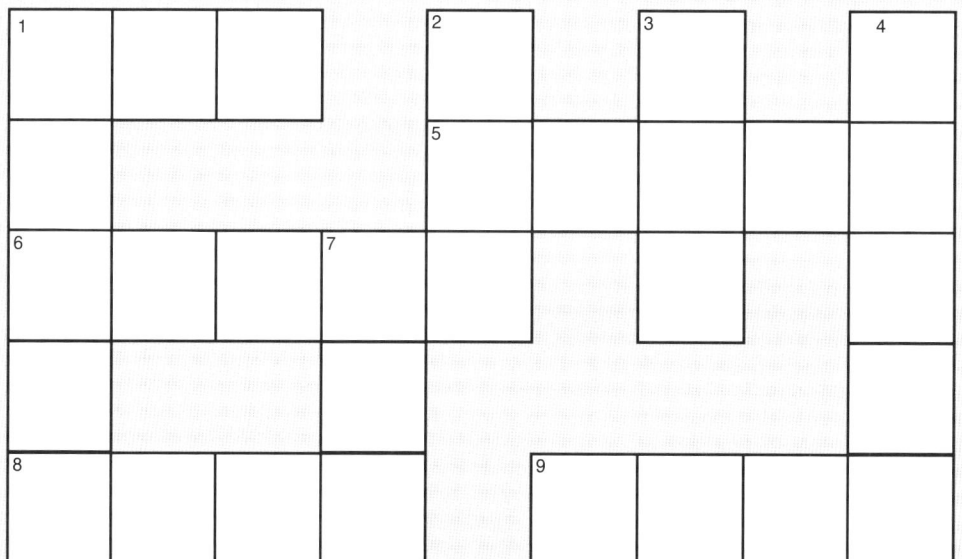

Antonym Crosswords

The answers are words which mean the opposite of the clues

Across:
1. right
4. cooked
5. command
6. sinks

Down:
1. plays
2. shrinks
3. stale

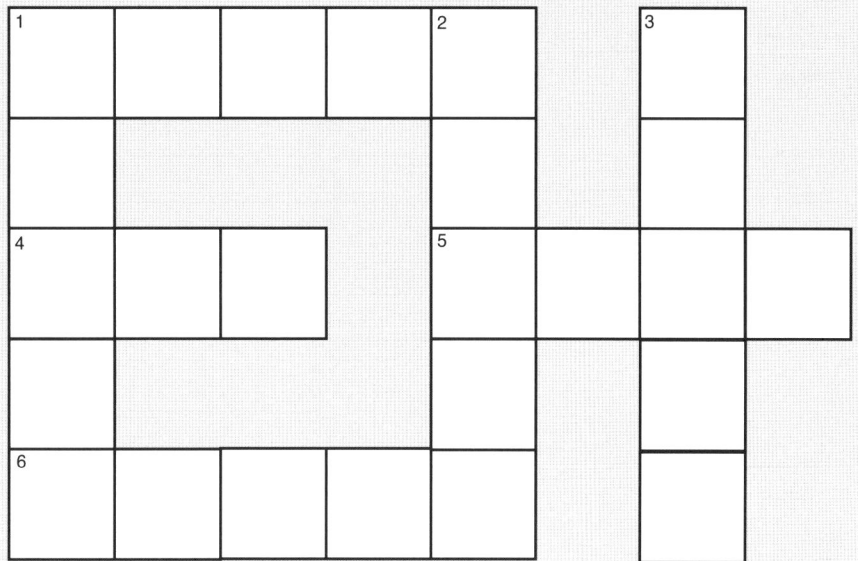

The answers are words which mean the opposite of the clues

Across:
1. backwards
5. tame
7. false

Down:
1. last
2. black
4. polite
6. blunt

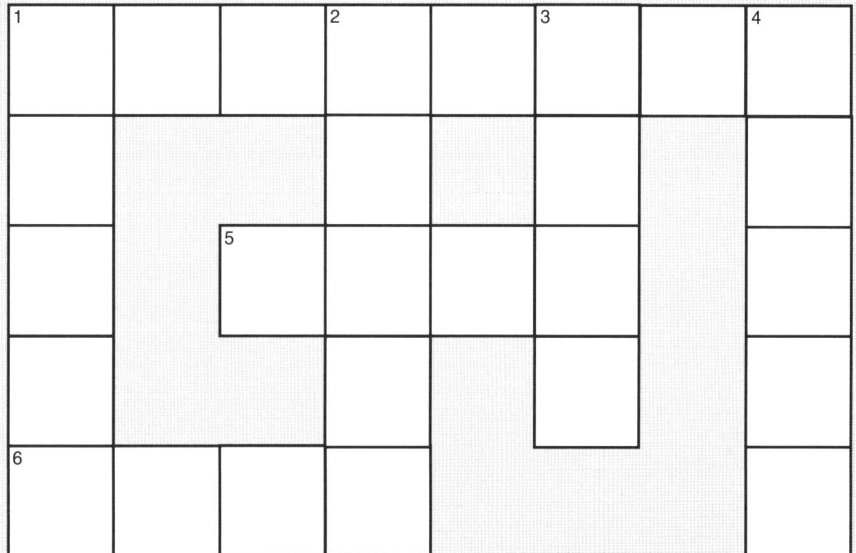

The answers are words which mean the opposite of the clues

Across:
1. forget
4. yes
5. happy
6. reply

Down:
1. poor
2. breaks
3. worst

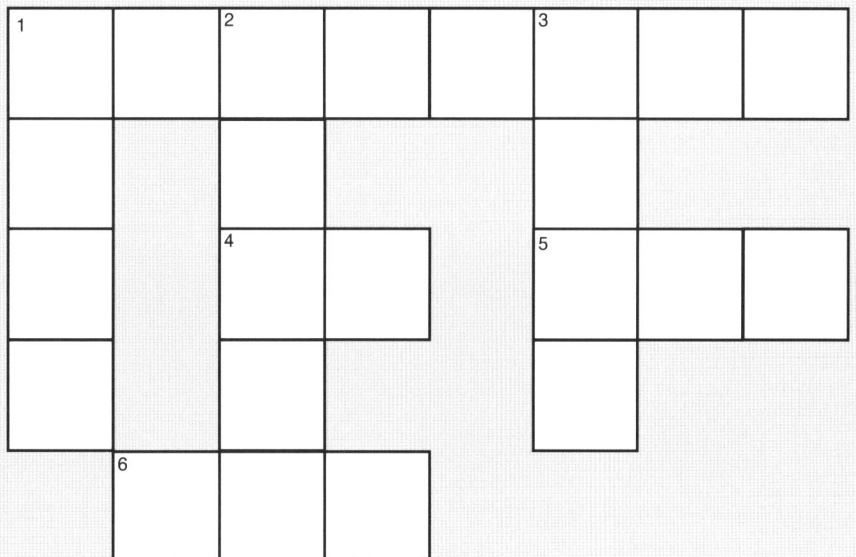

The answers are words which mean the same as the clues

Across:
1. centre
4. nothing
5. speak

Down:
1. shift
2. idle
3. near

The answers are words which mean the same as the clues

Across:
2. small
4. purchase
5. friends

Down:
1. glue
2. noisy
3. quick

The answers are words which mean the same as the clues

Across:
1. construct
4. above
5. chair

Down:
1. wide
2. big
3. stop

The answers are words which mean the same as the clues

Across:
1. robber
4. conceal
5. moist

Down:
1. narrow
2. discover
3. foe

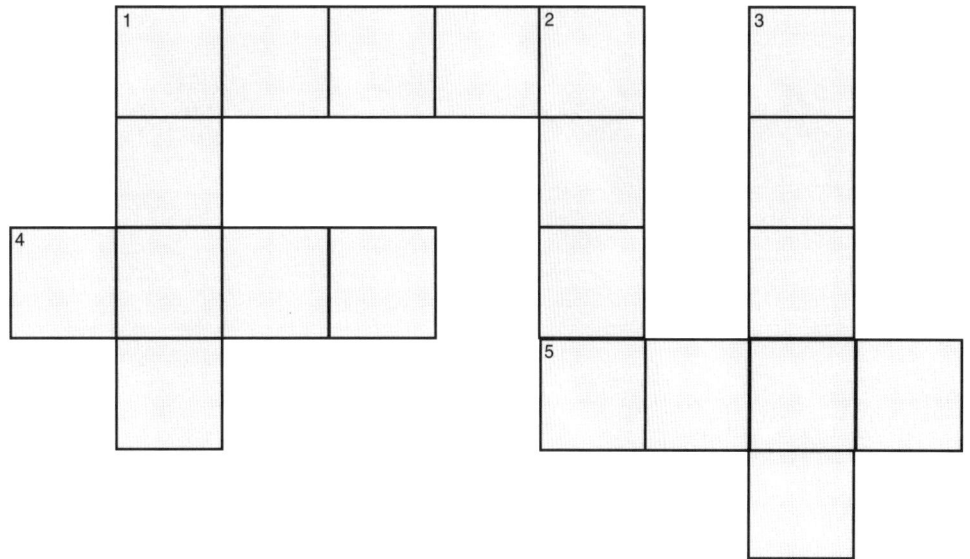

The answers are words which mean the same as the clues

Across:
1. certain
3. alter
5. weep

Down:
1. post
2. correct
4. difficult

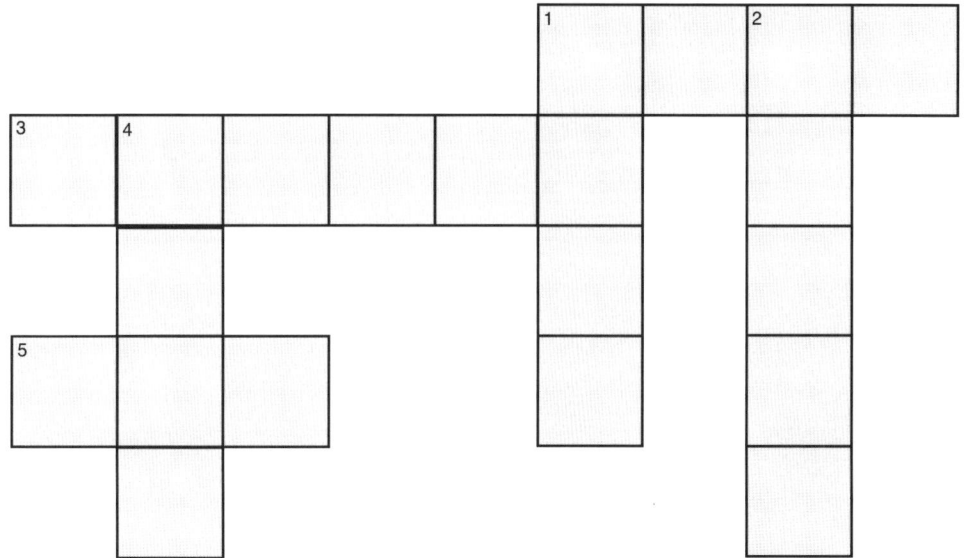

The answers are words which mean the same as the clues

Across:
1. answer
3. closed
5. under

Down:
1. circular
2. shout
4. pair

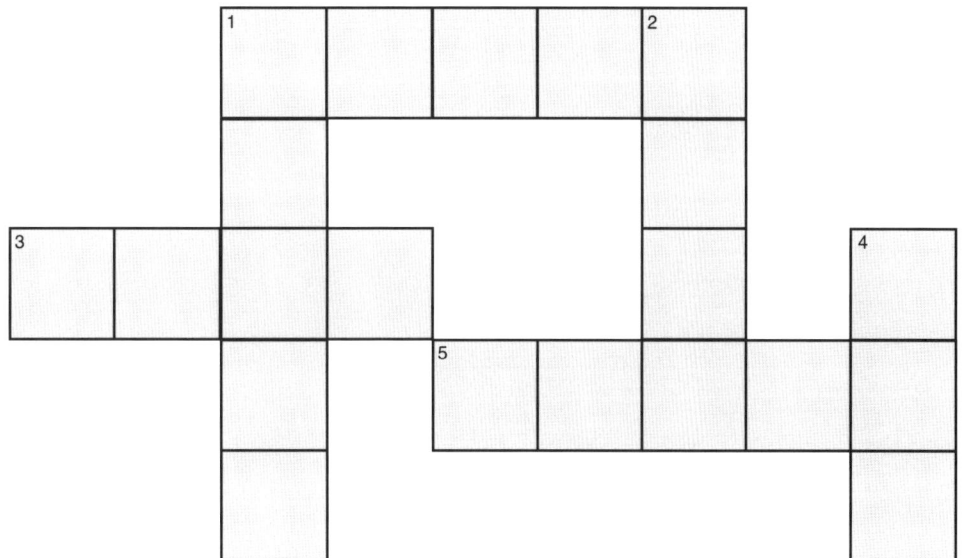

Antonym crosswords

page 138

Crossword 1:
```
e m p t y
a   e   e n d s
s t a y s   a
y   c     c r y
  w e a k   k
```

Crossword 2:
```
d i r t y
u   o     o
l o u d   d
l   g o o d
  h
```

Crossword 3:
```
o l d   b   a   a
p     u n d e r
e a r l y   d   g
n     o     u
s l o w   f r e e
```

page 139

Crossword 1:
```
w r o n g   f
o   r   r
r a w   o b e y
k     w   s
s w i m s   h
```

Crossword 2:
```
f o r w a r d s
i     h   u   h
r   w i l d   a
s     t   e   r
t r u e     p
```

Crossword 3:
```
r e m e m b e r
i   e     e
c   n o   s a d
h   d     t
  a s k
```

Synonym crosswords

page 140

Crossword 1:
```
m i d d l e   c
o     a   l
v   z e r o   o
e   s a y   s
              e
```

Crossword 2:
```
    s
l i t t l e   f
o   i     a
b u y   c h u m s
d   k     t
```

Crossword 3:
```
b u i l d
r   a   h
o v e r   a
a   g   l
d   s e a t
```

page 141

Crossword 1:
```
t h i e f   e
h   i   n
h i d e   n
n   d a m p
    y
```

Crossword 2:
```
    s u r e
c h a n g e   i
  a   n   g
c r y   d   h
r         t
```

Crossword 3:
```
r e p l y
o   e
s h u t   l
n   b e l o w   t
d         o
```

Pesky Pairs

Aim: To be able to describe the way two words are the same and how they are different.

Materials: Photocopy pages 144 -147 onto card and cut along the dotted lines. Laminate if possible.
Photocopy the game board on page 132.
One dice.
A counter for each player.

Game: Shuffle the cards and place face down on the table. Players take turns to pick a card and read the words on it. They then throw the dice and move around the board. If they land on a white square they have to say how the two items are the same, if on a black square they say how the items are different.

A page of blank cards has been included on page 148 so that additional items can be added as required.

kettle + teapot

jar + can

teeth + tusks

jet + rocket

towel + flannel

bracelet + watch

watch + clock

plane + helicopter

octopus + spider

spider + fly

snake + worm

jug + watering can

camel + kangaroo

swan + duck

sun + moon

frog + fish

pen + pencil

letter + postcard

bus + train

wall + fence

horse + cow

sheep + goat

bath + sink

rat + mouse

knife + fork

brush + toothbrush

monkey + gorilla

apple + pear

cup + mug

tiger + lion

plate + saucer

jumper + cardigan

fox + wolf

chair + sofa

door + window

nail + screw

collar + cuff

brush + comb

slug + snail

flower + tree

duck + chicken

lemon + melon

pupil + teacher

snake + eel

pen + printer

horns + antlers

paw + hoof

gate + fence

Similes

Aim: To complete well known similes.

Materials: Photocopy pages 150 -157 onto card and cut along the dotted lines. Laminate if possible.

Game: Shuffle the cards containing the beginning of the similes (pages 150 -153) and place in a pile face down on the table. Shuffle and deal out the end of the similes (pages 154 - 157) and deal out face up to the players. Players take turns to turn over the top card from the pile on the table, read the phrase and see if they have the phrase which completes the simile. If not, the card is placed face up on a discard pile and the next player can select this card or one from the pile. The winner is the player who has completed the most similes.

Alternatively this could be presented as a completion game when either the first or second part of the simile is read out loud and players are required to complete the simile. Players could be encouraged to suggest alternative endings to the similes.

A page of blank cards has been included on page 158 so that additional items can be added as required.

As bold as...

As green as...

As high as...

As hard as...

As soft as...

As old as...

As bright as...

As flat as...

As smooth as...

As sharp as...

As keen as...

As dull as...

As heavy as...

As poor as...

As bad as...

As busy as...

As tight as...

As quiet as...

As wobbly as...

As deaf as...

As cool as...

As fresh as...

As slippery as...

As thin as...

As black as...

As sober as...

As plain as...

As startled as...

As pretty as...

As white as...

As thick as...

As weak as...

As clear as...

As clean as...

As tough as...

As sly as...

As happy as...

As proud as...

As warm as...

As cold as...

As free as...

As right as...

As hungry as...

As fierce as...

As light as...

As neat as...

As good as...

As strong as...

...brass

...grass

...a kite

...nails

...butter

...the hills

...a button

...a pancake

...silk

...a needle

...mustard

...ditchwater

...lead

...a church mouse

...a rotten egg

...a bee

...drum

...a mouse

...a jelly

...a post

...a cucumber

...a daisy

...an eel

...a rake

...soot

...a judge

...as the nose on your face

...a rabbit

...a picture

...a sheet

...a plank

...water

...crystal

...a whistle

...old boots

...a fox

...a sandboy

...Punch

...toast

...ice

...a bird

...rain

...a horse

...a lion

...a feather

...a new pin

...gold

...an ox

Cool Concepts

Aim: The object of the game is to encourage players to name specific concepts in relation to given items.

Materials: Photocopy pages 161-163 onto card and cut along the dotted lines. Laminate if possible.
Photocopy the game board on page 160.

Game: A board game where players take turns to turn over a picture card and throw a dice to move around a board. Depending on which square they land on they either have to name:

a) Something in the same category as the item in the picture

b) something which has the same shape or colour

c) something which has the same use or function

d) Something made of the same material

Help can be given as required, and it may be advantageous to ask the player to verbalise his/her thinking, e.g. for cake - what is a cake made of? Now what else is made of these things?

A page of blank cards has been included on page 164 so that additional items can be added as required.

class

function

material

choose a concept

colour or shape

class

function

material

colour or shape

move back 5 places

material

colour or shape

class

move forward 5 places

material

move back 5 places

colour or shape

class

function

colour or shape

function

function

function

class

material

function

material

class

choose a concept

have another turn

change with another player

change with another player

colour or shape

colour or shape

colour or shape

material

material

class

function

material

class

function

class

function

END

function

material

function

class

colour or shape

move forward 5 places

function

colour or shape

have another turn

material

function

class

colour or shape

START

colour or shape

material

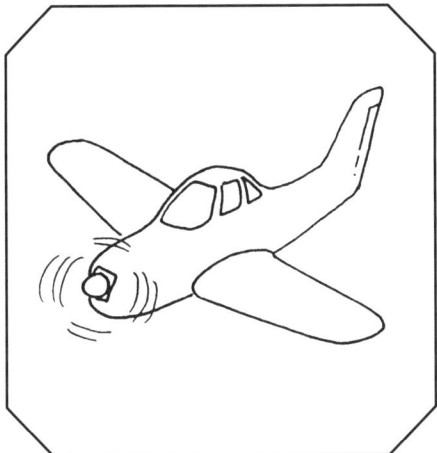

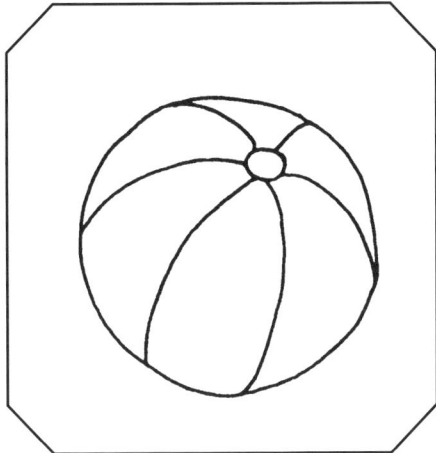

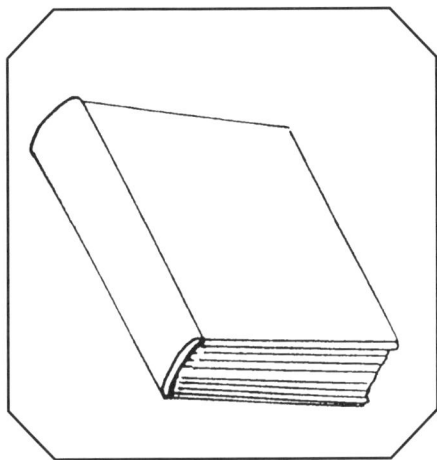

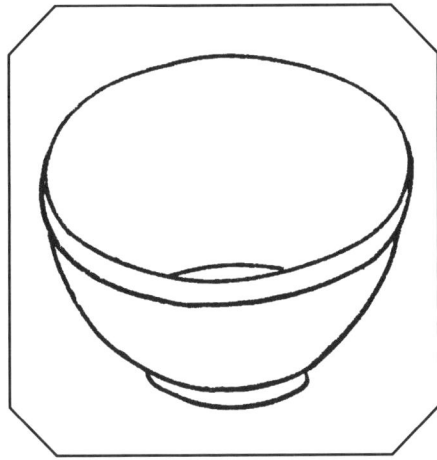

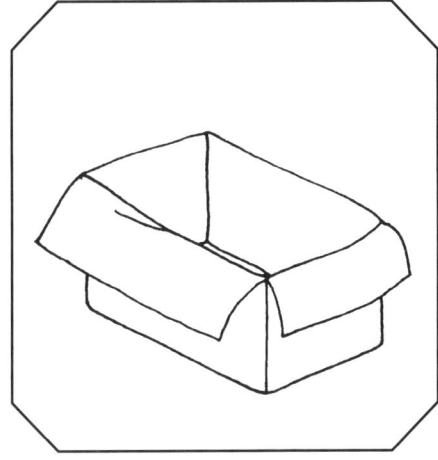

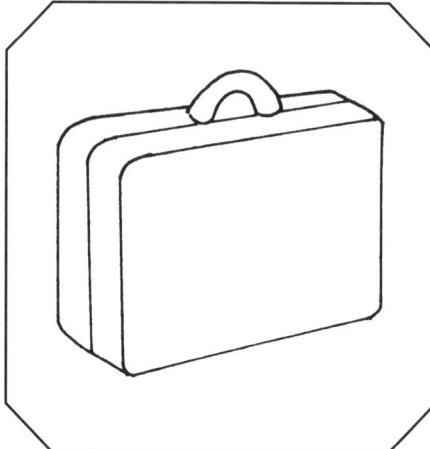

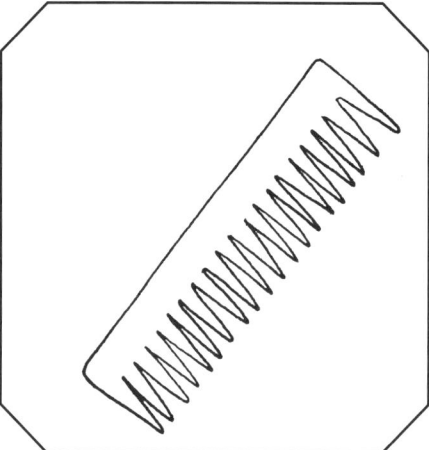
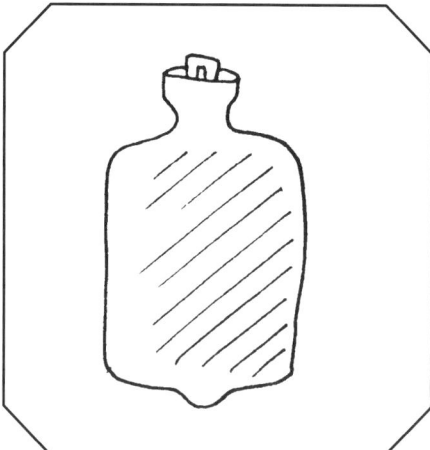
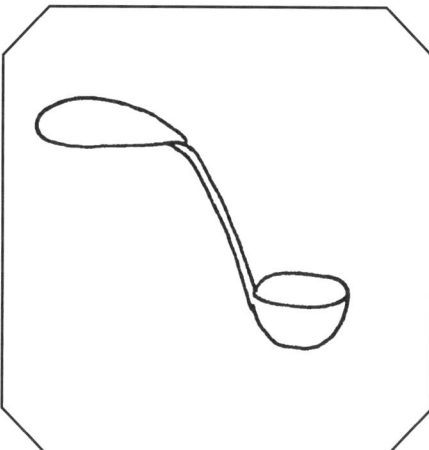

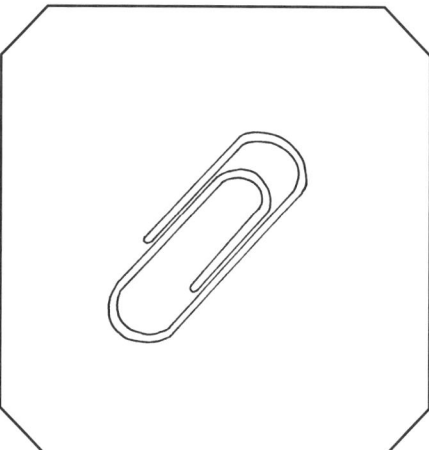

Cool Concepts

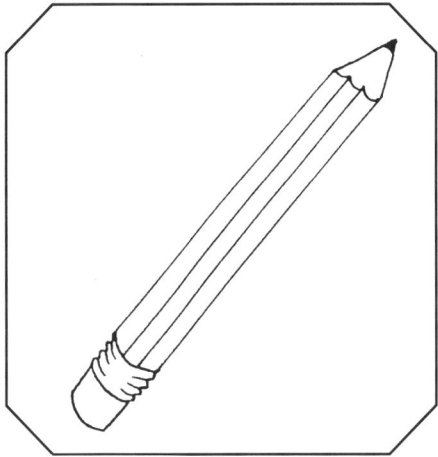

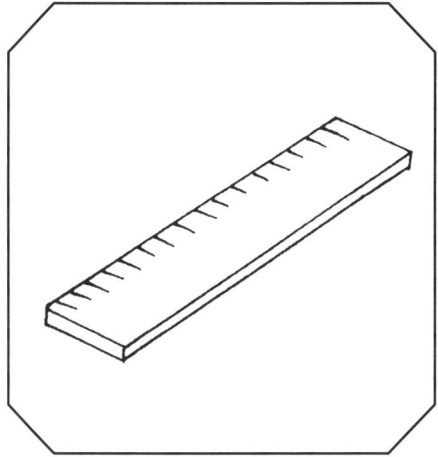
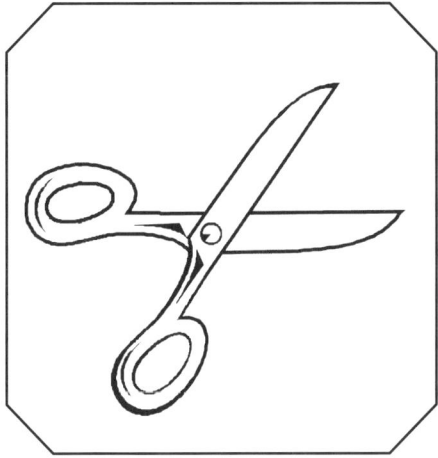
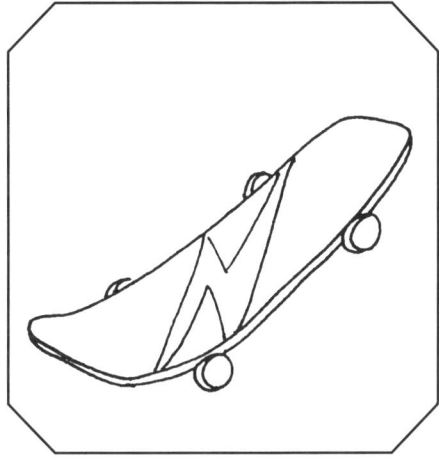
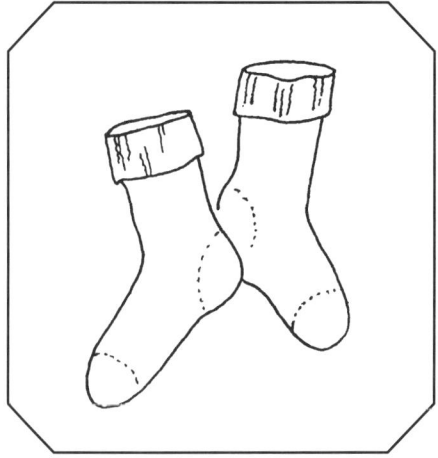

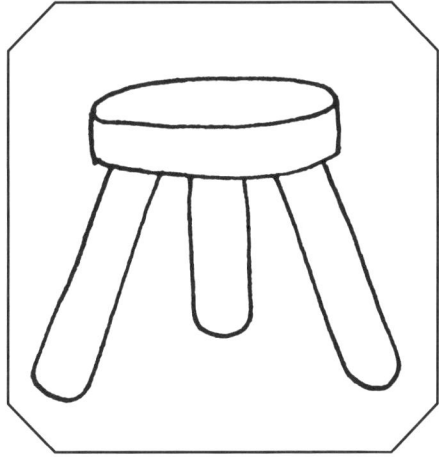

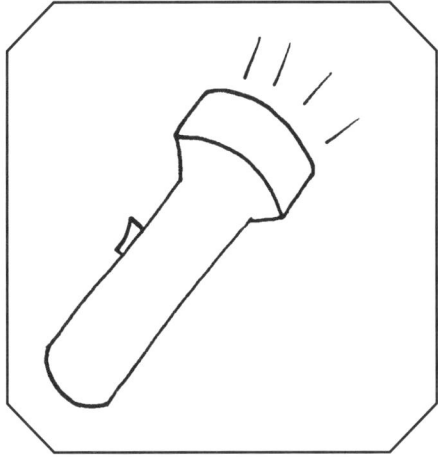
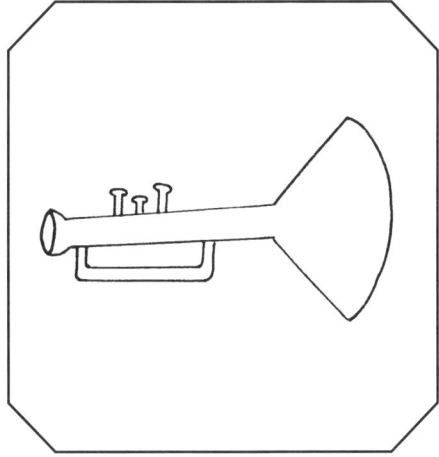
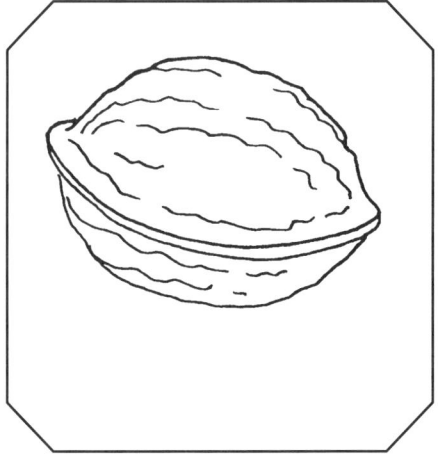

GAMES

The **RAILWAY, PIRATE, FANTASY, SPACE,** and **SAFARI** games are all straight forward board games. Throw a dice and move round the boards following the instructions as appropriate. It is suggested that the boards are enlarged to A3 size and laminated.

The **FOOTBALL** game is played with 2 dice. At the start, set a time limit for the game and appoint one player to keep the score. Players choose which of the two teams to play - if there are more than 2 players, they can divide equally between the teams. Players take it in turns to throw the dice add the numbers together, and the counter is moved between the numbered footballers according to the numbers of the dice. A goal is scored when a player throws a double (e.g. throws two 4's). All the football players except the goal keeper can score a goal. The winner is the one whose team scores the most goals.

The **HAUNTED HOUSE** game is for up to 4 players is played with 2 dice. Make a copy of the Haunted House and the cards on pages 172 - 173 for each player. Make one copy of the Bat cards on pages 174 - 175, cut along the dotted lines, stick onto card, and laminate. Place the small cards in piles on the table and give each player a Haunted House. Players take it in turns to throw the dice, add the numbers together, and collect a card with a corresponding number to complete their house. If a player throws a number for a picture which they already have, they can take a Bat Card and follow the instructions on it. The winner is the one who completes their Haunted House first.

The **DETECTIVE** game is for up to 6 players and is played with one dice. Photocopy the Crime board on page 176 and half of page 179 onto card for each player. Make one copy of pages 177 - 178 onto card and cut along the dotted lines. Laminate if possible. Place all the small cards in piles on the table, and give each player a Crime Board. Players then choose one of the 6 suspects and places him/her on their board. Players take it in turns to throw the dice and collect items of evidence to convict their suspect of the crime by taking a card with a corresponding number.There are 2 different items for each number, apart from 6, so players can choose e.g. a weapon or a disguise if they throw a 3, depending on what is already on their board. Players can collect the cards in any order. There is a choice of witness, weapon, escape vehicle, and loot. The winner is the first one to complete their Crime Board.

These games were designed by Susan Armstrong. The Pirate, Fantasy, Space, Football and Safari games are available as laminated boards in FULL COLOUR from STASS Publications in A3 size (approx. 41cms x, 29cms) or A2 size (approx. 58.5 cms x 41cms). A Game Pack is also available containing dice, shaker, counters, spinner and an egg timer). Telephone 01661 822316 for details.

Start

Throw an odd number to continue →

Station

Engine breakdown - miss a turn ↑

Signal at green - have another turn ↑

Track repairs - miss a turn →

Cow on line - go back 3 spaces

Terminus

Leaves on line - go back 2 spaces →

Shunt into siding and miss a turn →

Level Crossing

Throw 3 or 4 to continue

Red signal - throw even number to continue ↓

© STASS Publications 2001

166

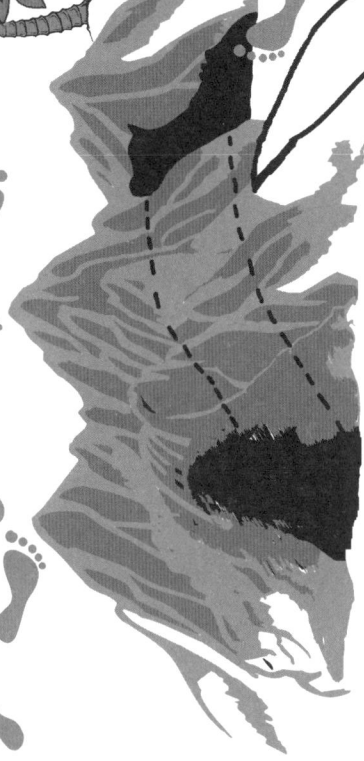

Throw an odd number to get through the forest

Throw a 4, 5 or 6 to go on through the tunnel

Throw a 1, 2 or 3 to cross the bridge

Finish

Throw 6 to fight off other pirates

Stop to explore the cave – miss a turn

Spy enemy ship– hurry forward 4 paces

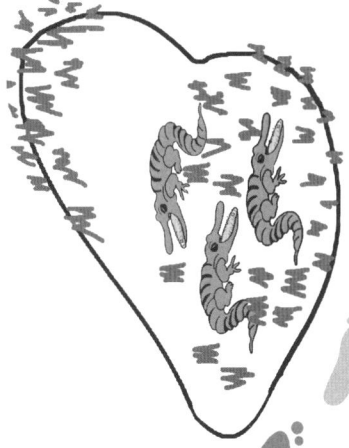

Stop for a rest – throw an even number to continue

Attacked by crocodiles! Change places with another player

Search for treasure map – go back 2 paces

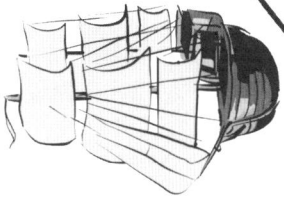

Start

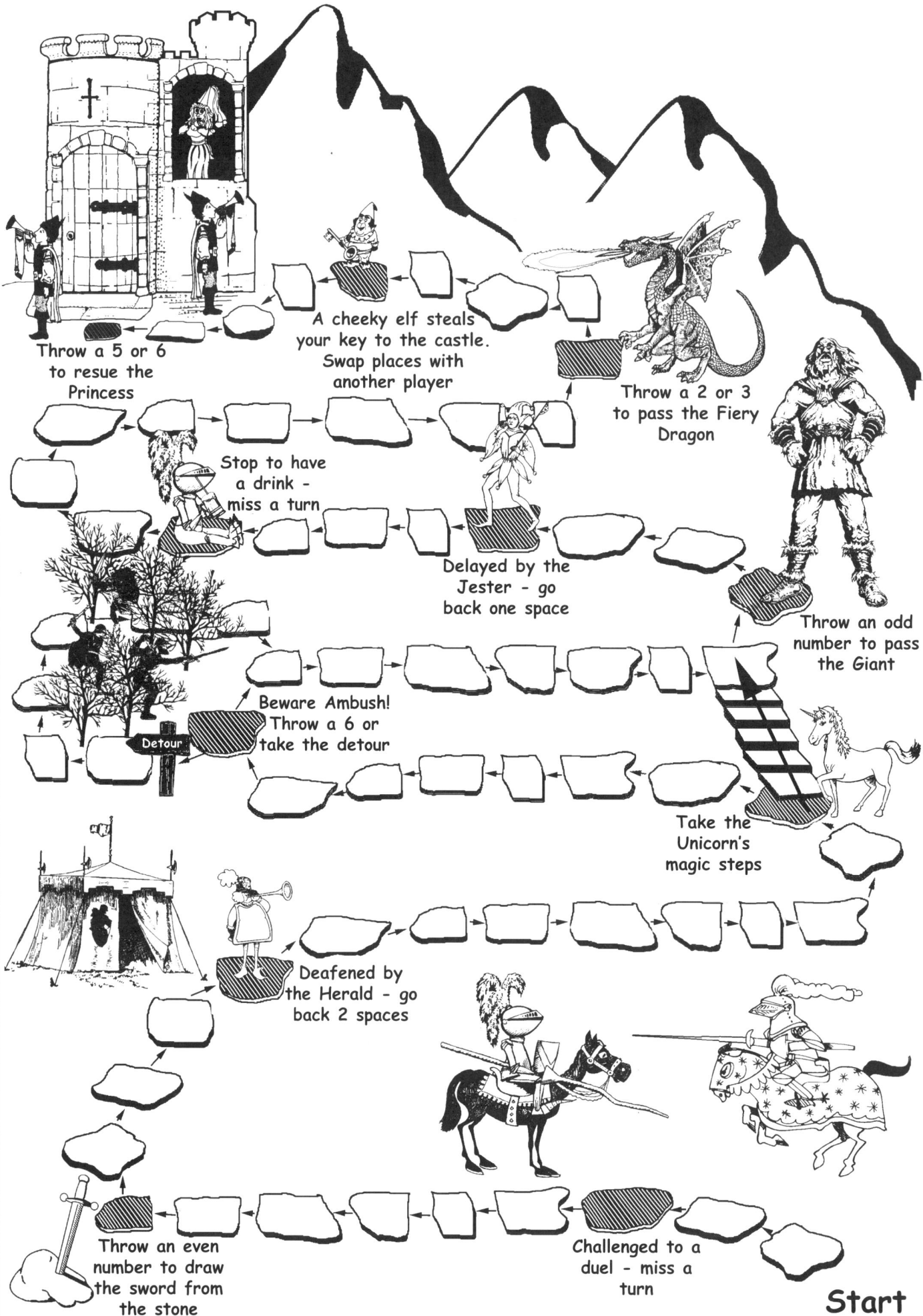

Throw a 5 or 6 to resue the Princess

A cheeky elf steals your key to the castle. Swap places with another player

Throw a 2 or 3 to pass the Fiery Dragon

Throw an odd number to pass the Giant

Stop to have a drink - miss a turn

Delayed by the Jester - go back one space

Beware Ambush! Throw a 6 or take the detour

Detour

Take the Unicorn's magic steps

Deafened by the Herald - go back 2 spaces

Throw an even number to draw the sword from the stone

Challenged to a duel - miss a turn

Start

Throw an even number to avoid being sucked into the Black Hole

Land on the planet to plant a flag

Throw an odd number to take off again

Turn on booster rocket - move forward 4 spaces

Running out of oxygen - hurry - forward 2 places

Stop to take a space walk - miss a turn

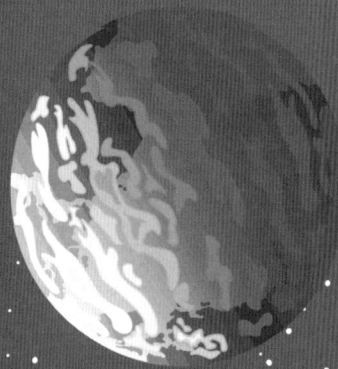

Hit by meteor - Go back 2 places

Aborted launch Return to Start

Land on the planet to collect some rock samples

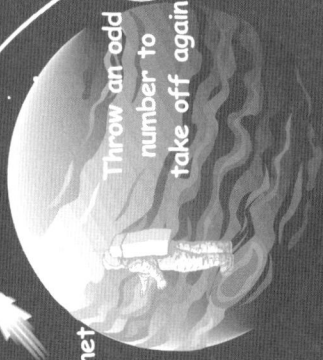

Throw an odd number to take off again

Start

End

© STASS Publications 2001

169

Start

Beware of lion – move back one place

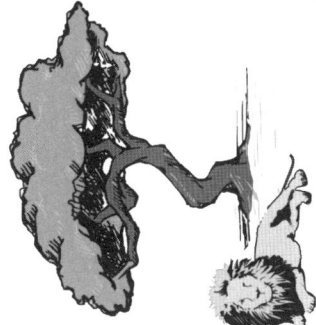

Make camp for the night – miss a turn

Stop to photograph zebras – throw a 2, 3 or 4 to continue

Frightened gazelles – move on 1 place

Admire the giraffe – throw a 1, 2 or 3 to continue

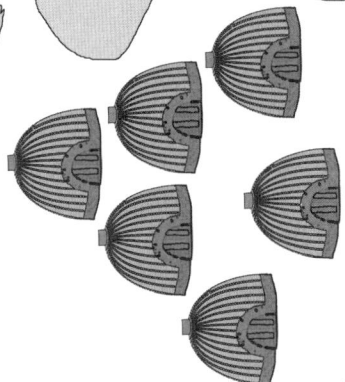

Angry rhino! move on 3 places

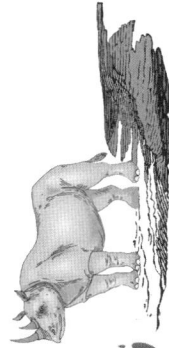

Hungry leopard – run back 3 spaces

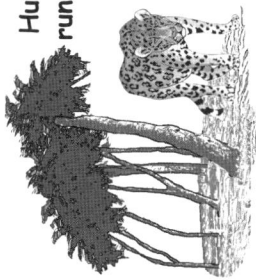

Visit village – miss a turn

Throw an odd number to cross the river

Elephants on the move – throw an even number to continue

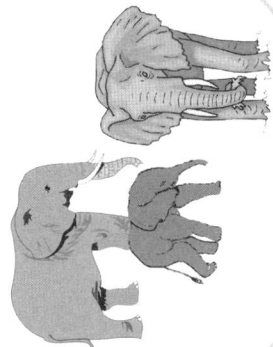

Finish

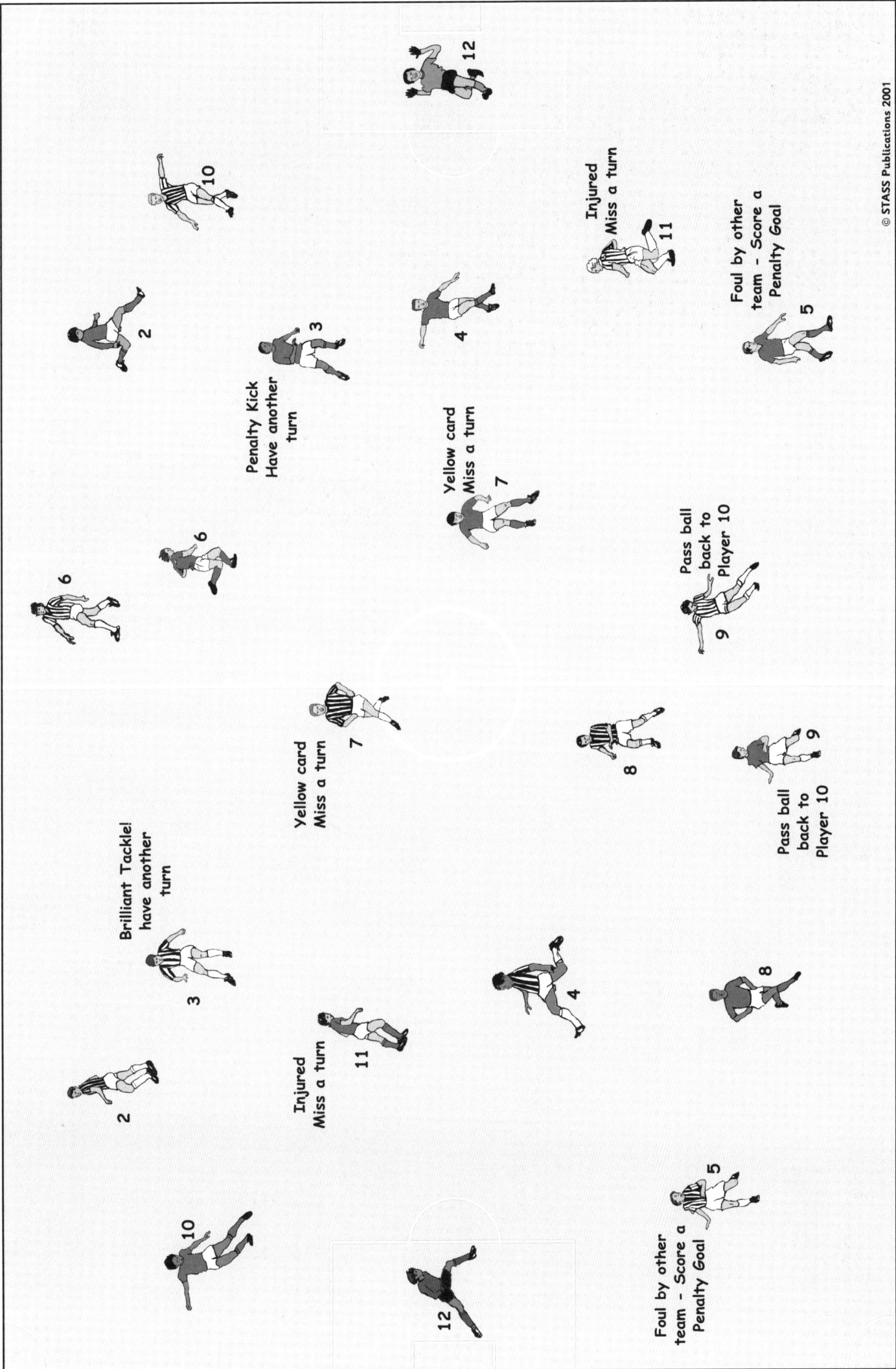

12

10

Injured
Miss a turn
11

Foul by other
team - Score a
Penalty Goal
5

2

3

4

Penalty Kick
Have another
turn

Yellow card
Miss a turn
7

6

6

Pass ball
back to
Player 10
9

Yellow card
Miss a turn
7

8

Pass ball
back to
Player 10
9

Brilliant Tackle!
have another
turn
3

2

Injured
Miss a turn
11

4

8

10

12

Foul by other
team - Score a
Penalty Goal
5

2

3 4 5

6 7 8

9 10 11

12

2

3

4

5

6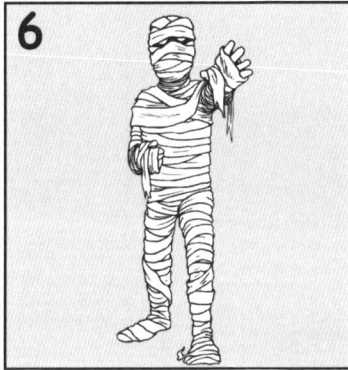

7

8

9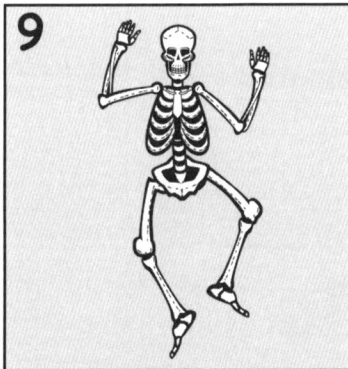

10

11

12

Spill the poison - swap a card with another player

Caught in the Spider's web - miss a turn

The owl flies off - take a free game card

Dracula laughs - swap a card with another player

Hide from the butler - miss a turn

Hear the skeleton laughing - throw the dice again

Chased by the ghost - put one of your game cards back

The cauldron boils over - throw the dice again

The mummy wakes up - miss a turn

See the lucky black cat - take a free game card

Frankenstein roars - put one of your game cards back

The Wizard has cast a spell - throw the dice again

The owl hoots - put one of your game cards back

Stir the cauldron - swap a card with another player

Hide from Dracula - miss a turn

The skeleton rattles - take a free game card

The Wizard is coming - put one of your game cards back

The mummy groans - swap a card with another player

The butler is coming - throw the dice again

Hear footsteps - take a free game card

Incident No. 1536 Robbery at Bartholemews Bank, Friday 13th August

SUSPECT	1 Escape Vehicle	4 Fingerprint
3 Weapon	5 CCTV	2 Witness
4 Loot	3 Disguise	1 Forged Passport
2 Identity Parade	5 Confession	6 Arrest

Detective Game

Suspect Frightful Freda	**Suspect** Dodgy Dan	**Suspect** Gruesome Gertrude	**Suspect** Eric the Eel
Suspect Wiley Will	**Suspect** Dangerous Delia	Weapon	Weapon
Weapon	Weapon	Weapon	Weapon
Escape Vehicle	Escape Vehicle	Escape Vehicle	Escape Vehicle

Escape Vehicle

Escape Vehicle

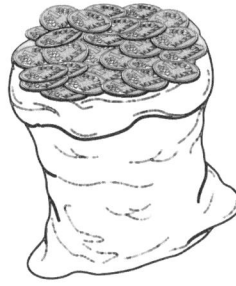

Loot

Loot

Loot

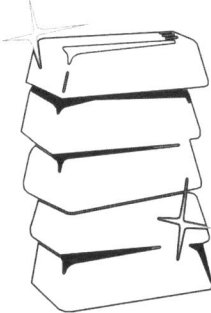

Loot

Loot

Loot

Witness

Mike the Messenger

Witness

Percy the Painter

Witness

Pat the Pensioner

Witness

Sally the Schoolgirl

Witness

Shiela the Shopper

Witness

Tessa the Taxi Driver

CCTV

Confession

Disguise

Fingerprint

Arrest

Forged Passport

Identity Parade

CCTV

Confession

Disguise

Fingerprint

Arrest

Forged Passport

Identity Parade

Copy half of
this page for
each player

PASSPORT

PASSPORT